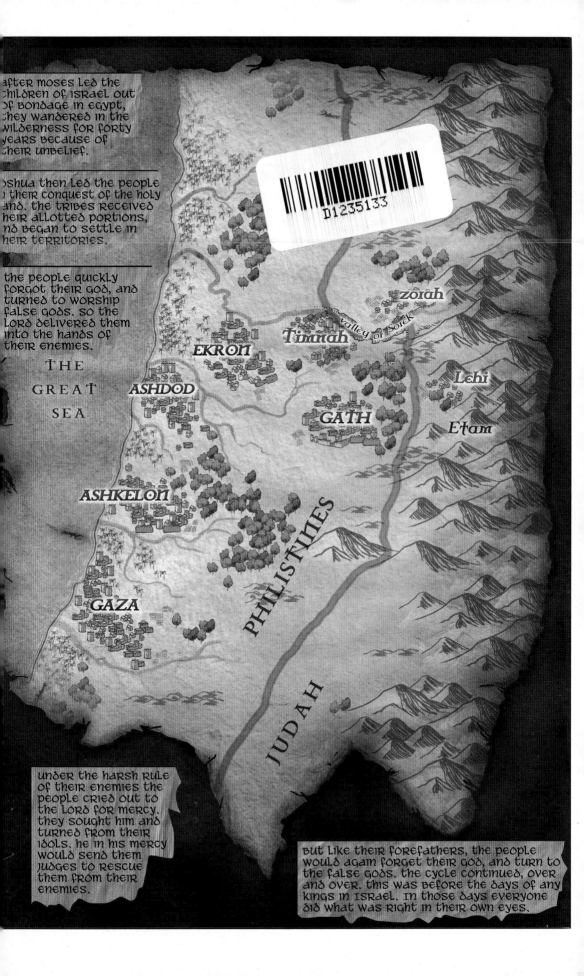

after moses led the children of israel out of bondage in egypt, they wandered in the wilderness for forty years because of their unbelief.

joshua then led the people in their conquest of the holy land. the tribes received their allotted portions, and began to settle in their territories.

the people quickly forgot their god, and turned to worship false gods. so the lord delivered them into the hands of their enemies.

THE GREAT SEA

EKRON

ASHDOD

Timnah

Valley of Sorek

zorah

Lehi

GATH

Etam

ASHKELON

PHILISTINES

GAZA

JUDAH

under the harsh rule of their enemies the people cried out to the lord for mercy. they sought him and turned from their idols. he in his mercy would send them judges to rescue them from their enemies.

but like their forefathers, the people would again forget their god, and turn to the false gods. the cycle continued, over and over. this was before the days of any kings in israel. in those days everyone did what was right in their own eyes.

~1100 B.C.

"Now the sons of Israel again did evil in the eye
of the Lord, so that the Lord gave them into the
hands of the Philistines for forty years"

– The Book of Judg

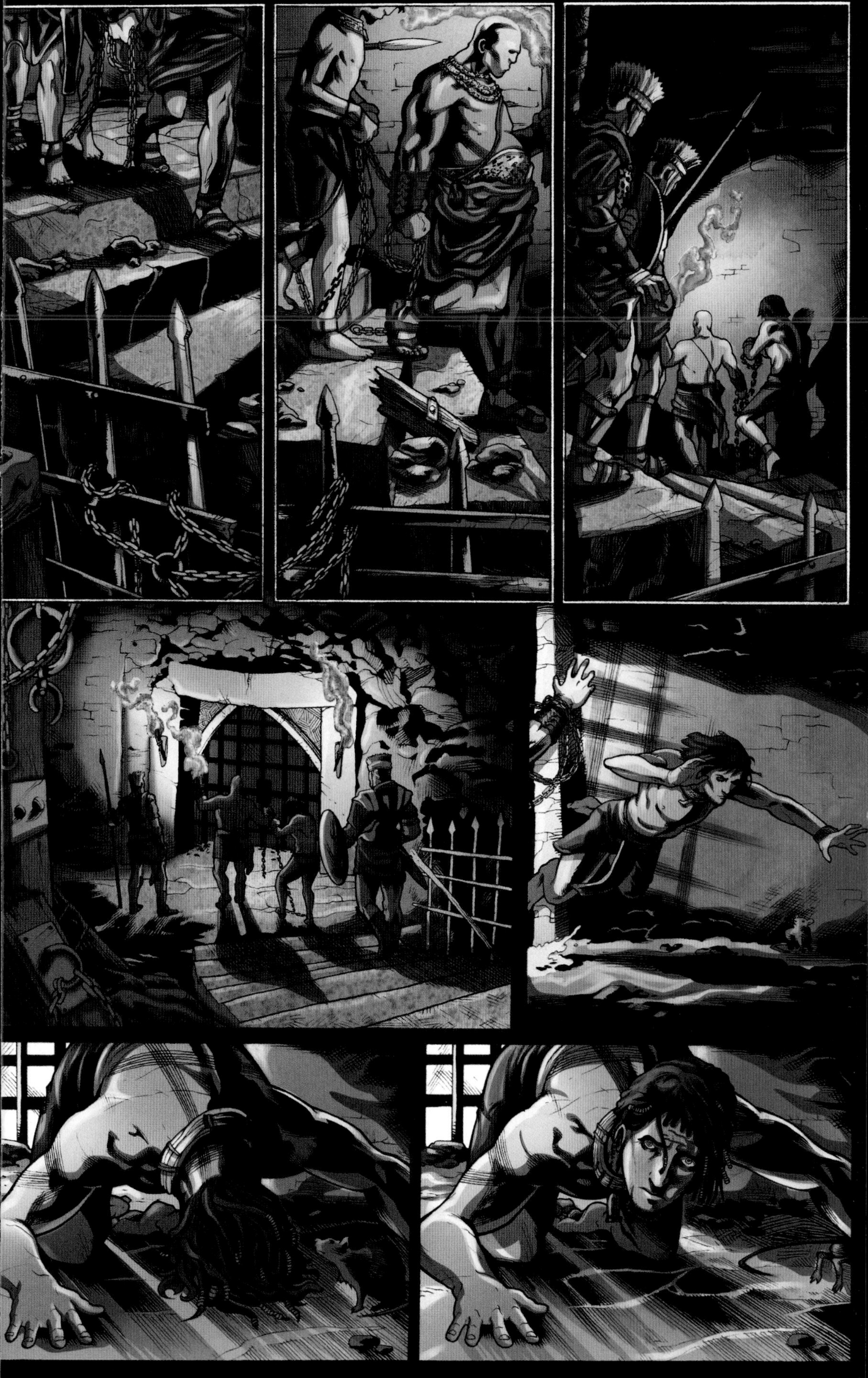

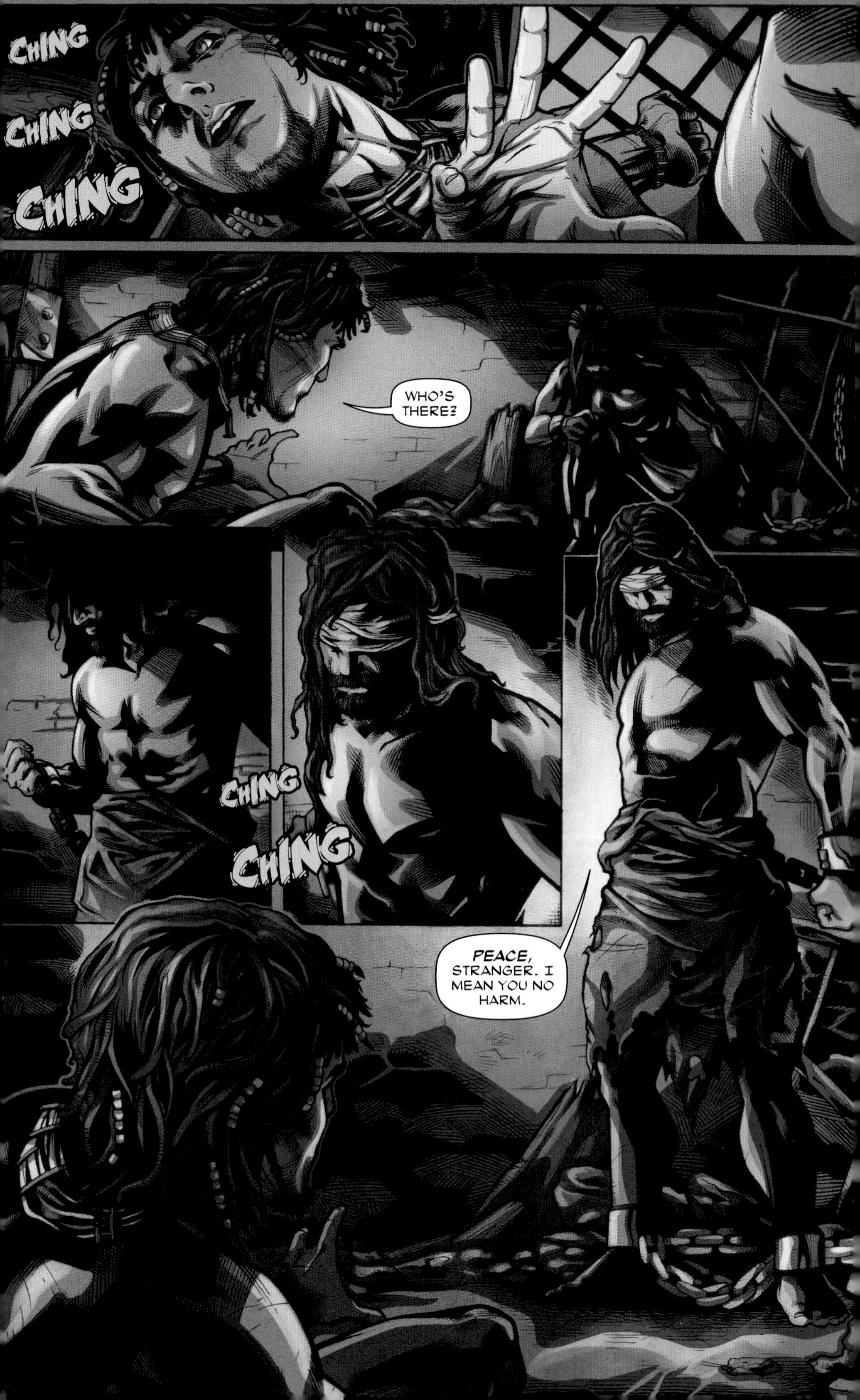
CHING
CHING
CHING
WHO'S THERE?
CHING
CHING
PEACE, STRANGER. I MEAN YOU NO HARM.

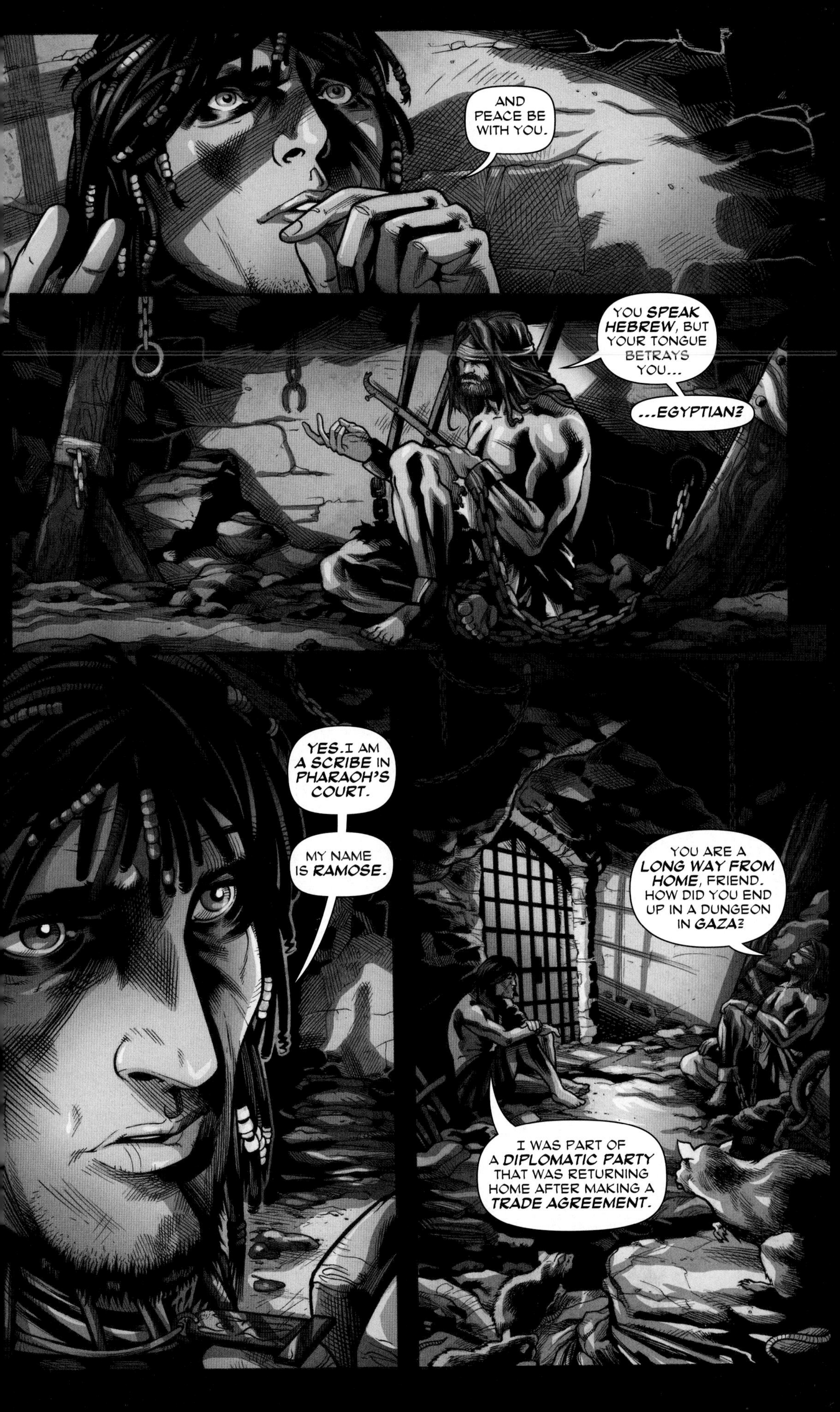
AND PEACE BE WITH YOU.
YOU SPEAK HEBREW, BUT YOUR TONGUE BETRAYS YOU...
...EGYPTIAN?
YES. I AM A SCRIBE IN PHARAOH'S COURT.
MY NAME IS RAMOSE.
YOU ARE A LONG WAY FROM HOME, FRIEND. HOW DID YOU END UP IN A DUNGEON IN GAZA?
I WAS PART OF A DIPLOMATIC PARTY THAT WAS RETURNING HOME AFTER MAKING A TRADE AGREEMENT.

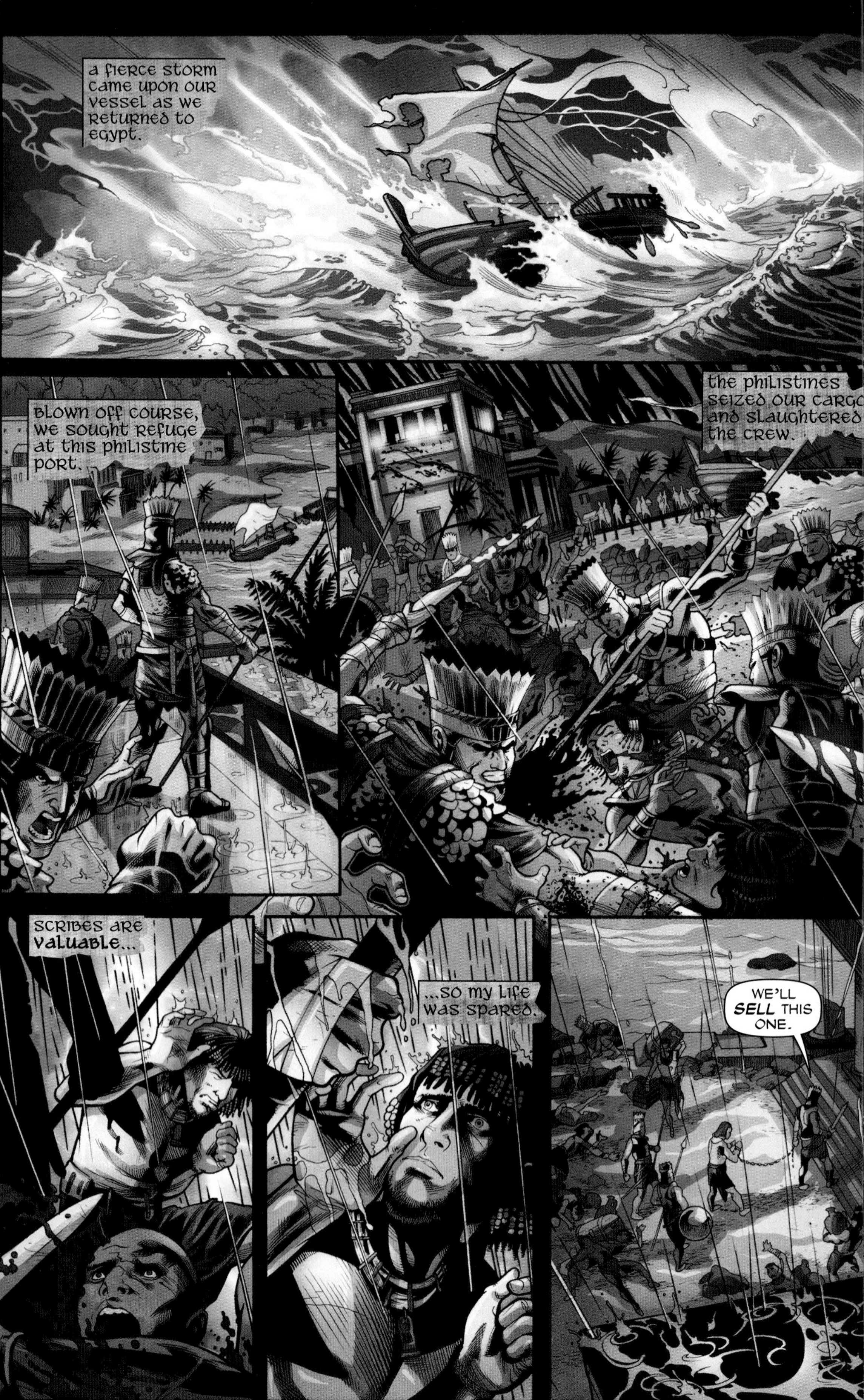
a fierce storm came upon our vessel as we returned to egypt.
blown off course, we sought refuge at this philistine port.
the philistines seized our cargo and slaughtered the crew.
scribes are valuable...
...so my life was spared.
WE'LL SELL THIS ONE.

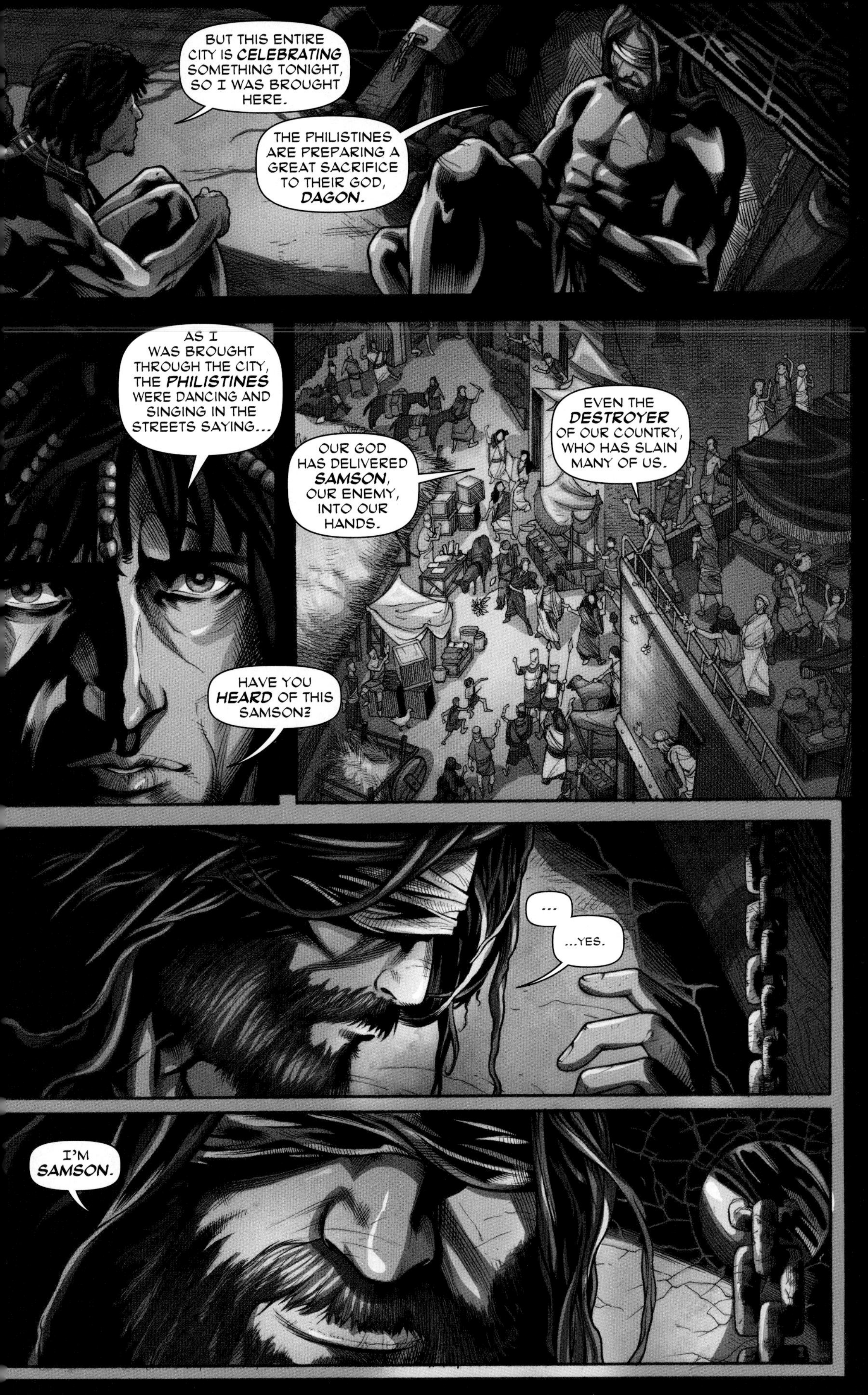
BUT THIS ENTIRE CITY IS CELEBRATING SOMETHING TONIGHT, SO I WAS BROUGHT HERE.
THE PHILISTINES ARE PREPARING A GREAT SACRIFICE TO THEIR GOD, DAGON.
AS I WAS BROUGHT THROUGH THE CITY, THE PHILISTINES WERE DANCING AND SINGING IN THE STREETS SAYING...
OUR GOD HAS DELIVERED SAMSON, OUR ENEMY, INTO OUR HANDS.
EVEN THE DESTROYER OF OUR COUNTRY, WHO HAS SLAIN MANY OF US.
HAVE YOU HEARD OF THIS SAMSON?
...
...YES.
I'M SAMSON.

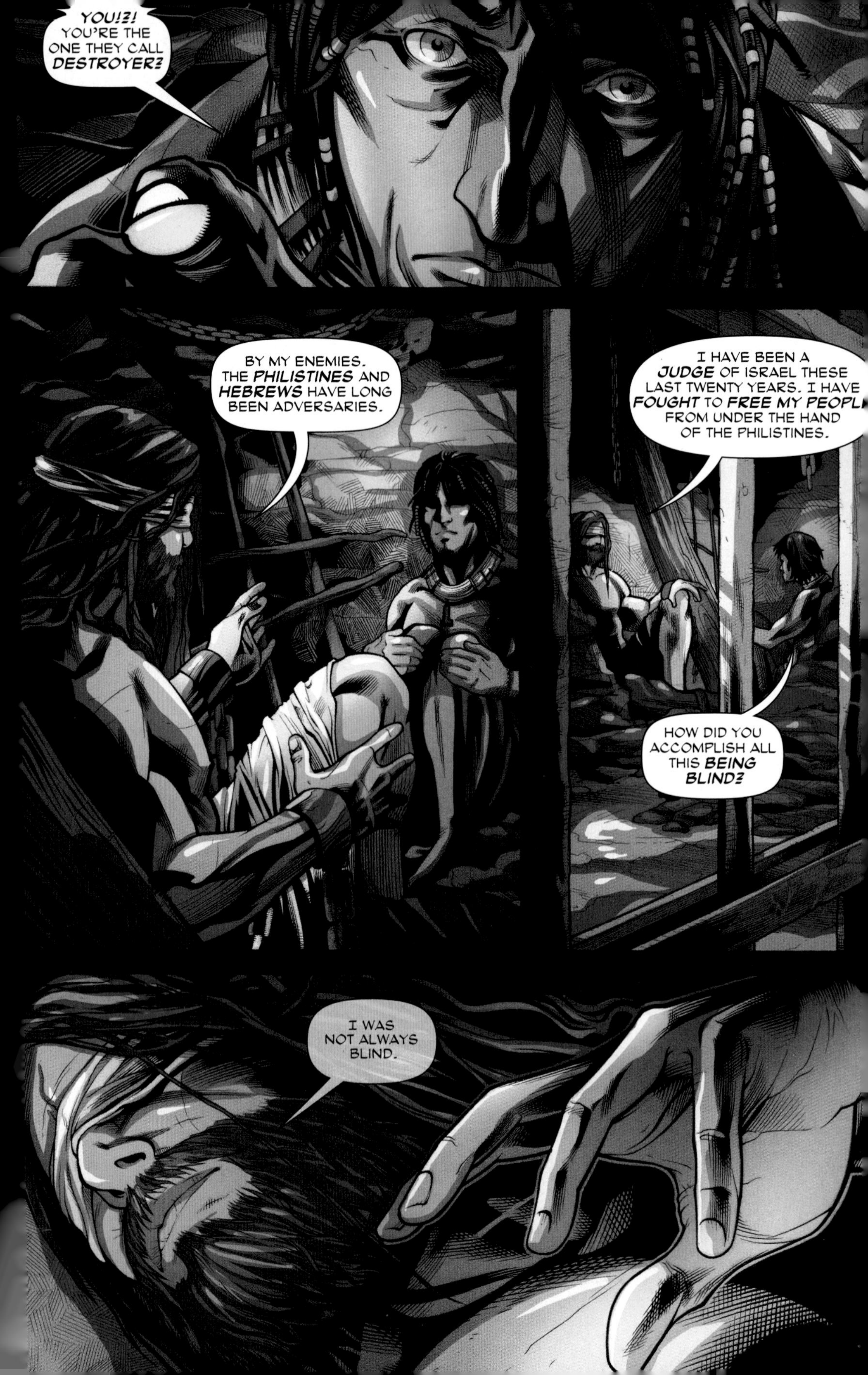
YOU!?! YOU'RE THE ONE THEY CALL DESTROYER?
BY MY ENEMIES. THE PHILISTINES AND HEBREWS HAVE LONG BEEN ADVERSARIES.
I HAVE BEEN A JUDGE OF ISRAEL THESE LAST TWENTY YEARS. I HAVE FOUGHT TO FREE MY PEOPL FROM UNDER THE HAND OF THE PHILISTINES.
HOW DID YOU ACCOMPLISH ALL THIS BEING BLIND?
I WAS NOT ALWAYS BLIND.

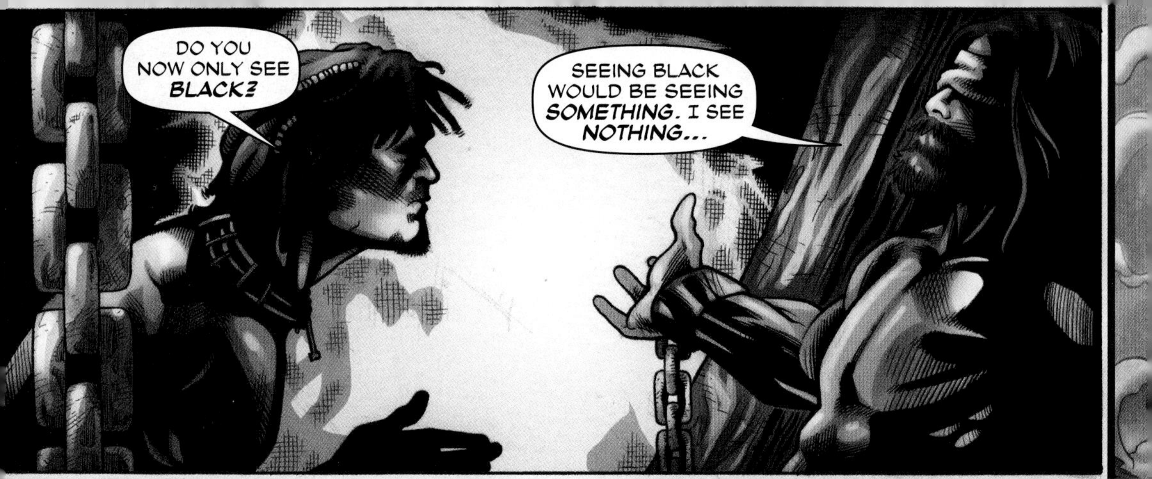
DO YOU NOW ONLY SEE BLACK?
SEEING BLACK WOULD BE SEEING SOMETHING. I SEE NOTHING...

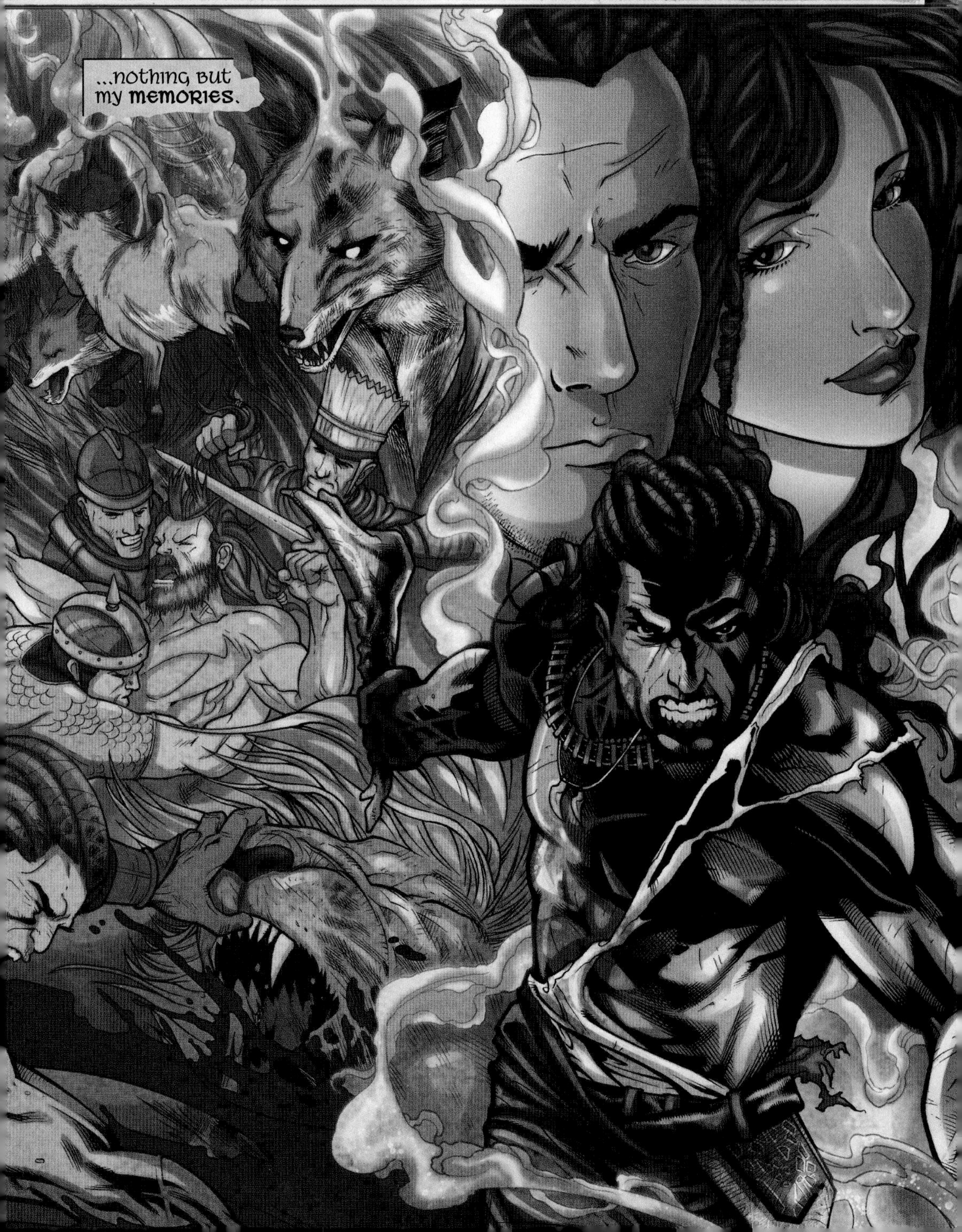
...nothing but my MEMORIES.

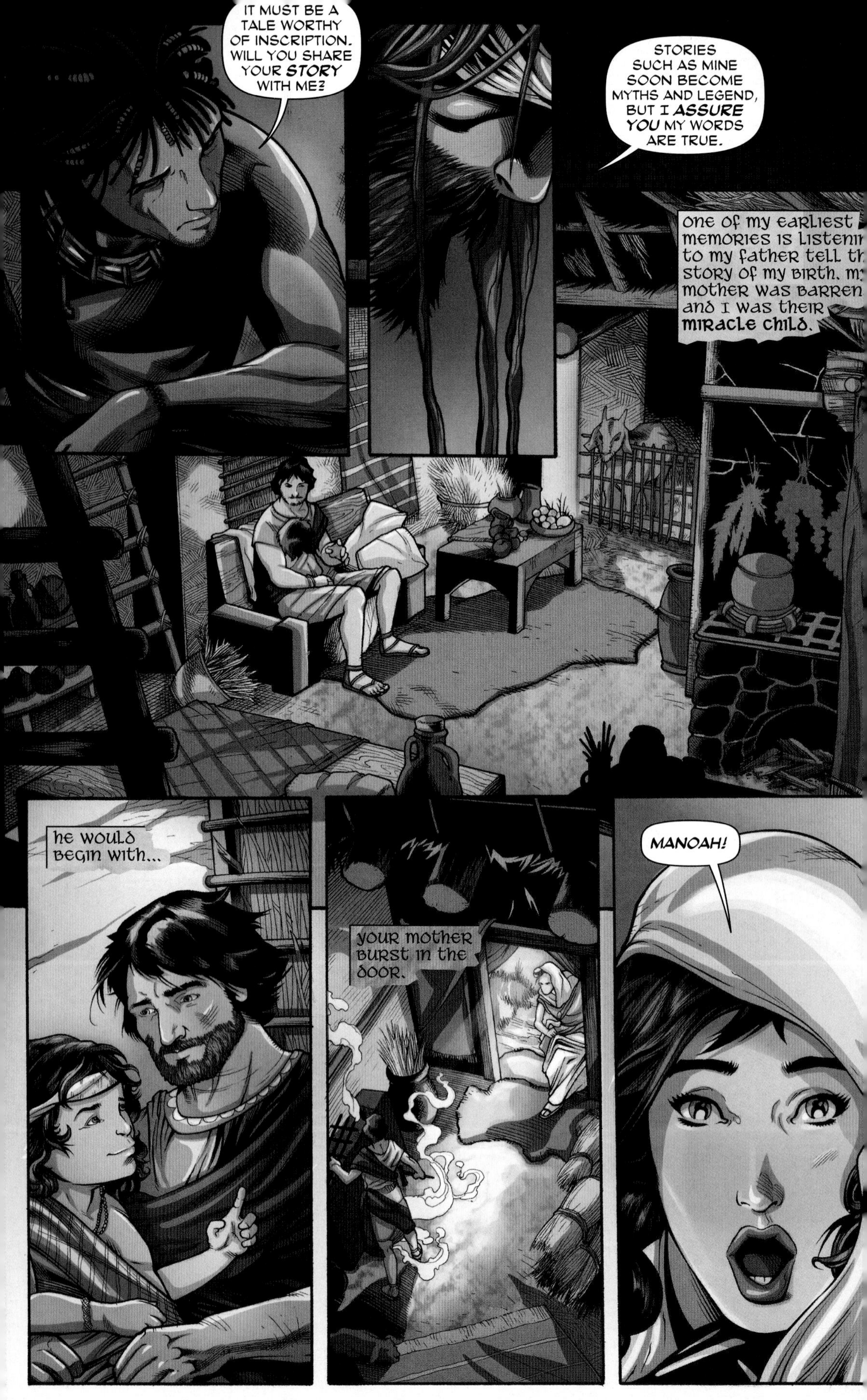
IT MUST BE A TALE WORTHY OF INSCRIPTION. WILL YOU SHARE YOUR STORY WITH ME?
STORIES SUCH AS MINE SOON BECOME MYTHS AND LEGEND, BUT I ASSURE YOU MY WORDS ARE TRUE.
one of my earliest memories is listenin to my father tell th story of my birth. m mother was barren and I was their miracle child.
he would begin with...
your mother burst in the door.
MANOAH!

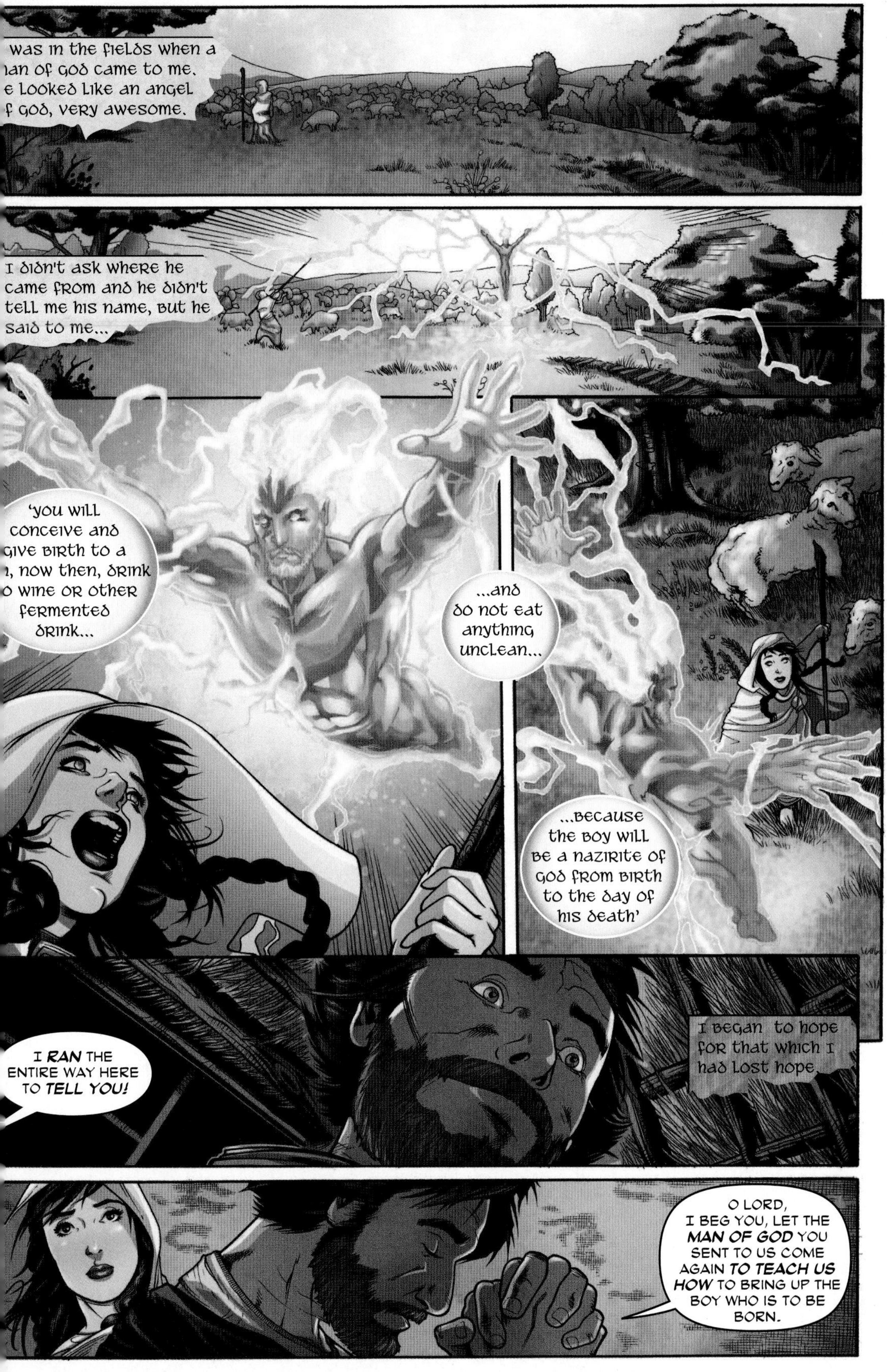
was in the fields when a an of god came to me. e looked like an angel f god, very awesome.
I didn't ask where he came from and he didn't tell me his name, but he said to me...
'you will conceive and give birth to a , now then, drink o wine or other fermented drink...
...and do not eat anything unclean...
...because the boy will be a nazirite of god from birth to the day of his death'
I RAN THE ENTIRE WAY HERE TO TELL YOU!
I began to hope for that which I had lost hope.
O LORD, I BEG YOU, LET THE MAN OF GOD YOU SENT TO US COME AGAIN TO TEACH US HOW TO BRING UP THE BOY WHO IS TO BE BORN.

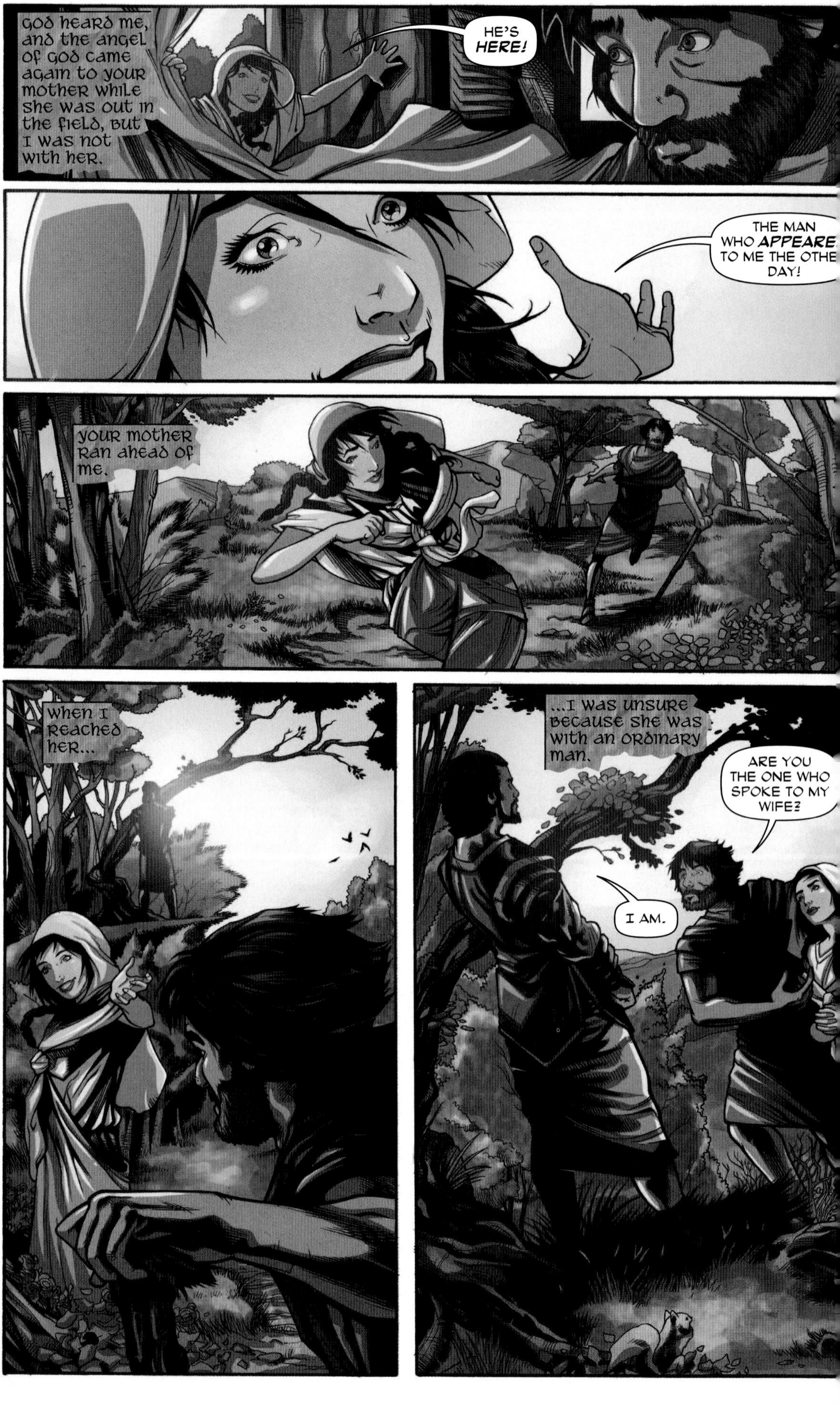
God heard me, and the angel of God came again to your mother while she was out in the field, but I was not with her.
HE'S HERE!
THE MAN WHO APPEARE TO ME THE OTHE DAY!
your mother Ran ahead of me.
when I Reached her...
...I was unsure because she was with an ordinary man.
ARE YOU THE ONE WHO SPOKE TO MY WIFE?
I AM.

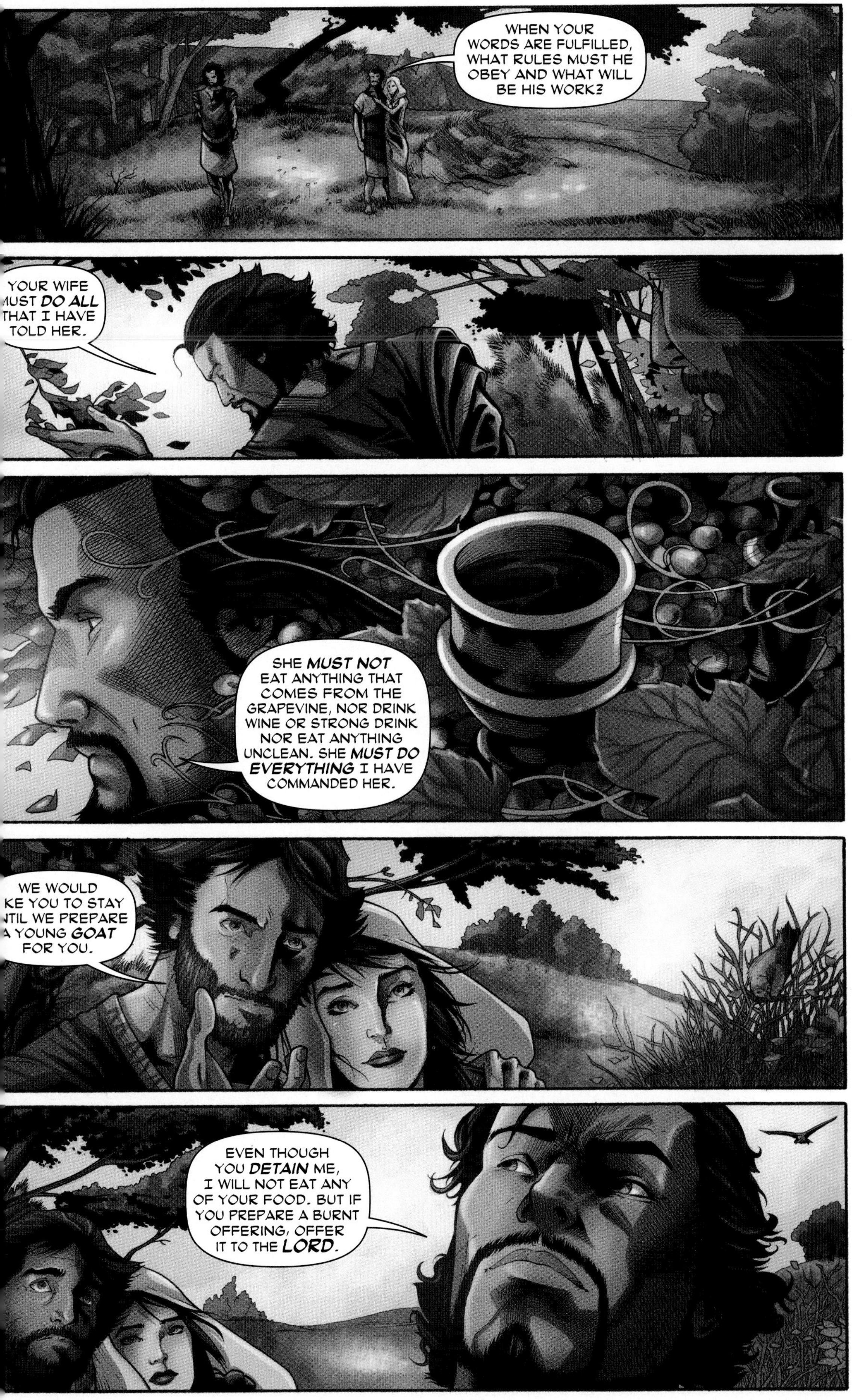

WHEN YOUR WORDS ARE FULFILLED, WHAT RULES MUST HE OBEY AND WHAT WILL BE HIS WORK?
YOUR WIFE UST DO ALL THAT I HAVE TOLD HER.
SHE MUST NOT EAT ANYTHING THAT COMES FROM THE GRAPEVINE, NOR DRINK WINE OR STRONG DRINK NOR EAT ANYTHING UNCLEAN. SHE MUST DO EVERYTHING I HAVE COMMANDED HER.
WE WOULD KE YOU TO STAY NTIL WE PREPARE YOUNG GOAT FOR YOU.
EVEN THOUGH YOU DETAIN ME, I WILL NOT EAT ANY OF YOUR FOOD. BUT IF YOU PREPARE A BURNT OFFERING, OFFER IT TO THE LORD.

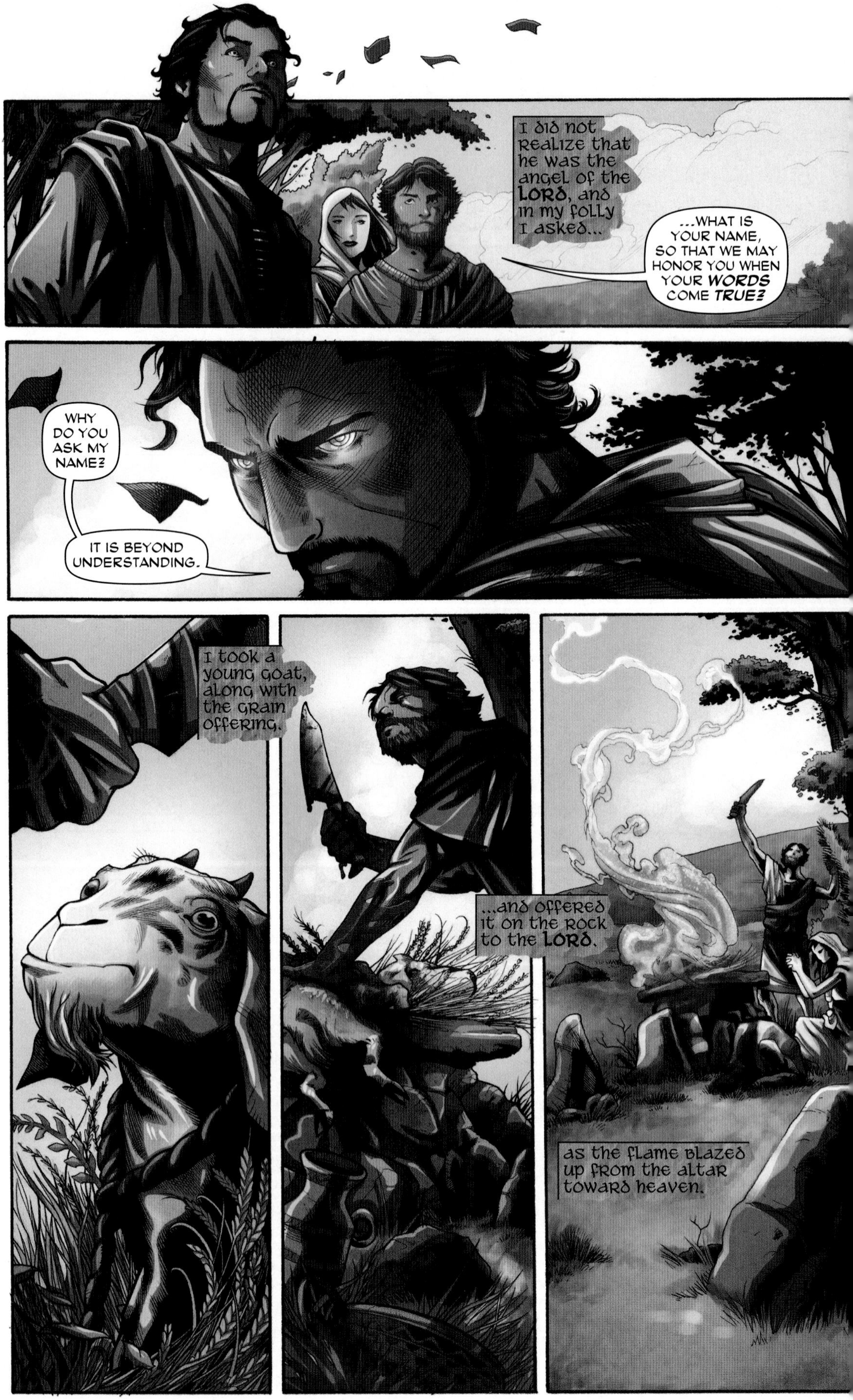
I did not realize that he was the angel of the LORD, and in my folly I asked...
...WHAT IS YOUR NAME, SO THAT WE MAY HONOR YOU WHEN YOUR WORDS COME TRUE?
WHY DO YOU ASK MY NAME?
IT IS BEYOND UNDERSTANDING.
I took a young goat, along with the grain offering,
...and offered it on the rock to the LORD,
as the flame blazed up from the altar toward heaven.

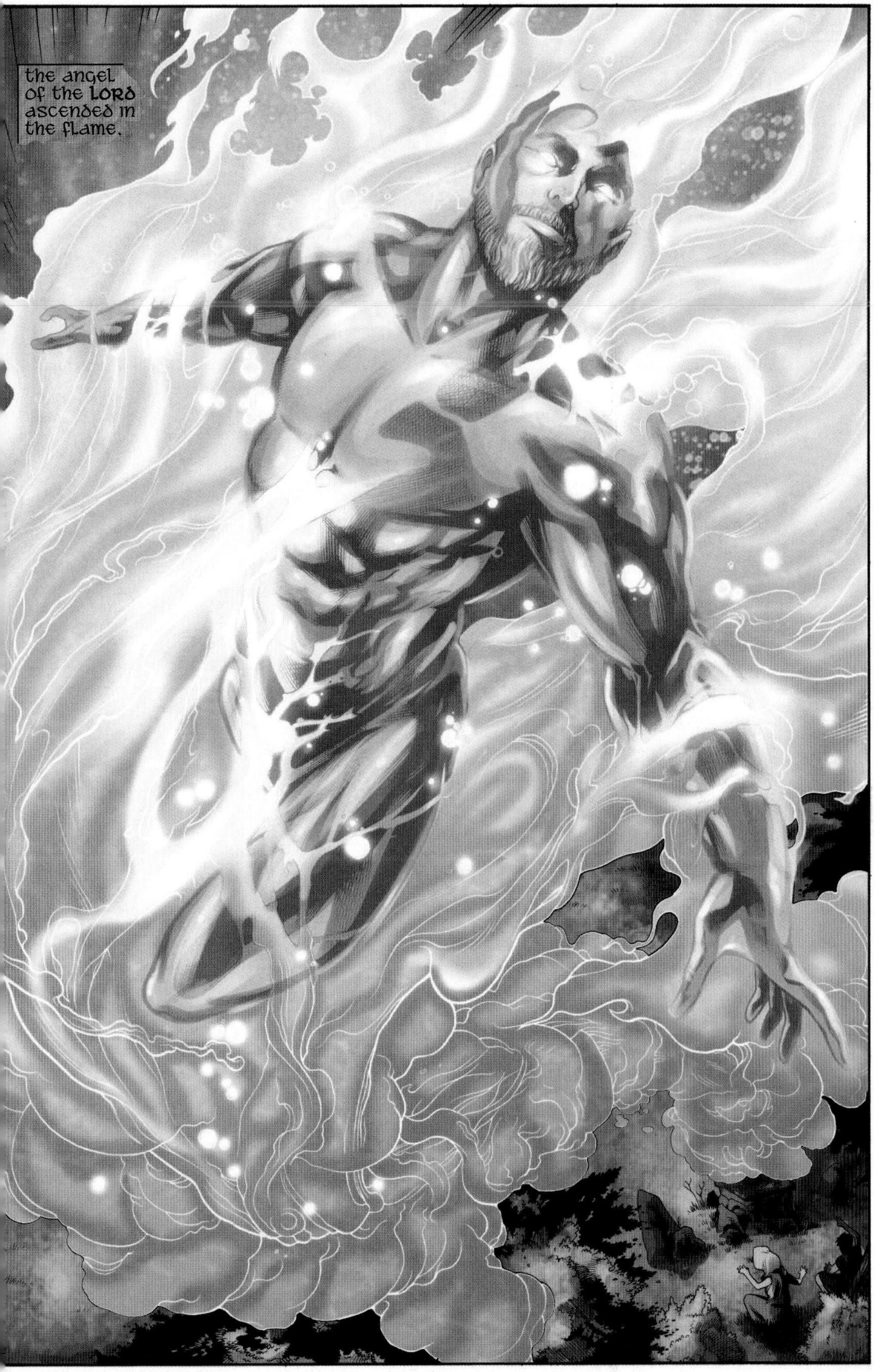
the angel of the LORD ascended in the flame.

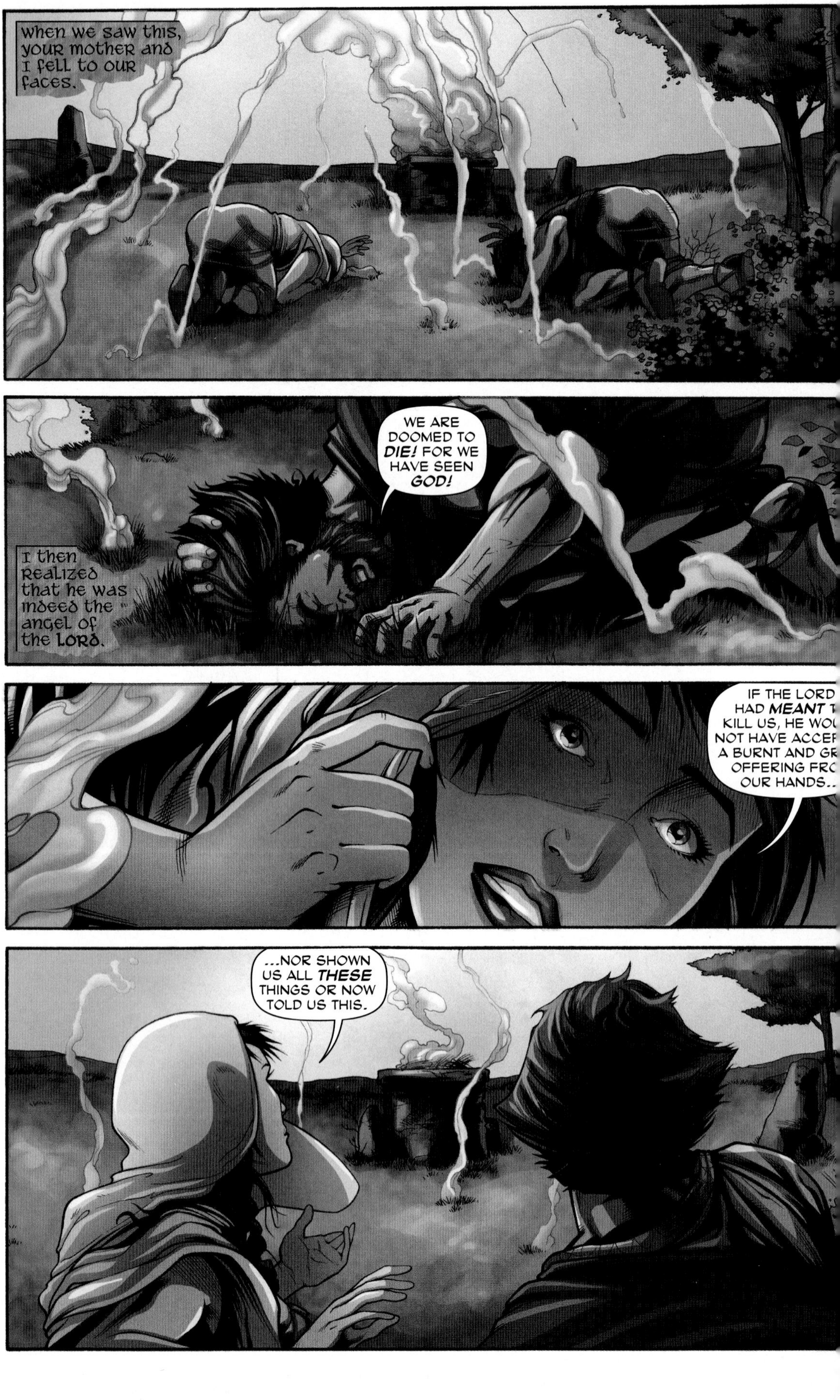
when we saw this, your mother and I fell to our faces.
WE ARE DOOMED TO DIE! FOR WE HAVE SEEN GOD!
I then realized that he was indeed the angel of the LORD.
IF THE LORD HAD MEANT T KILL US, HE WOU NOT HAVE ACCEP A BURNT AND GR OFFERING FRO OUR HANDS..
...NOR SHOWN US ALL THESE THINGS OR NOW TOLD US THIS.

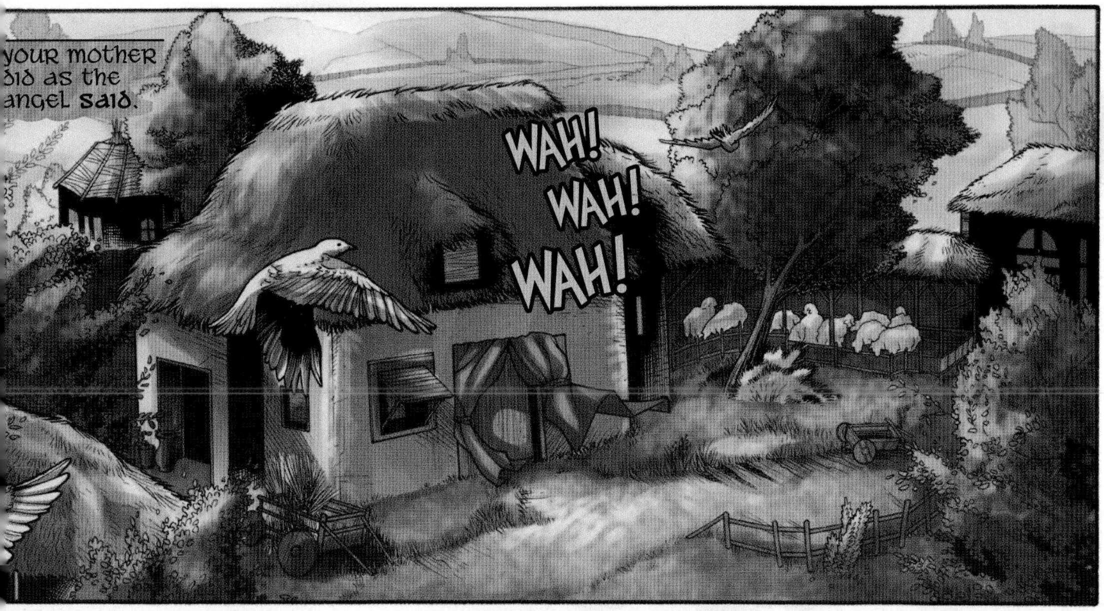
your mother did as the angel said.
WAH! WAH! WAH!

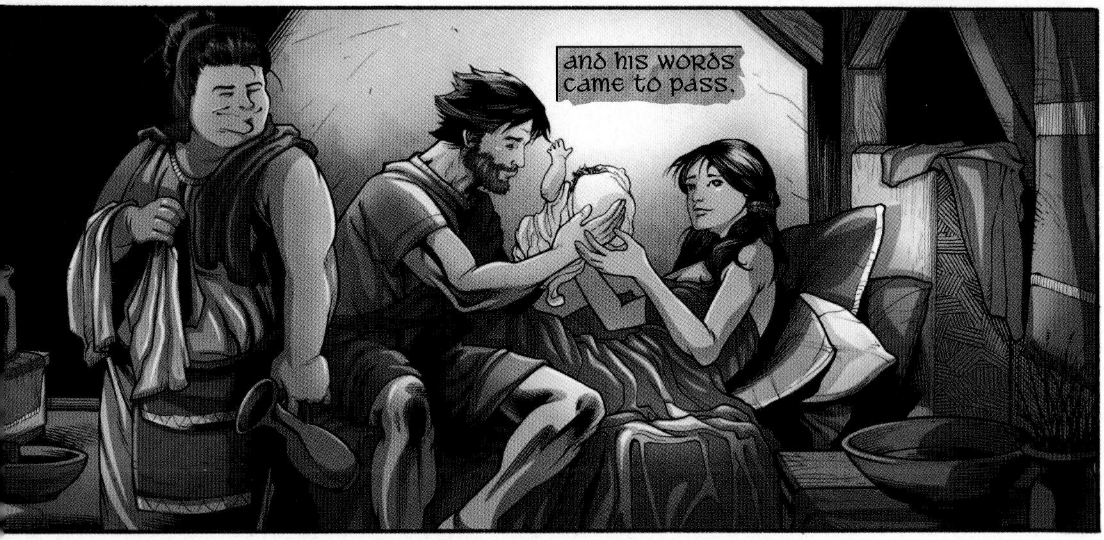
and his words came to pass.

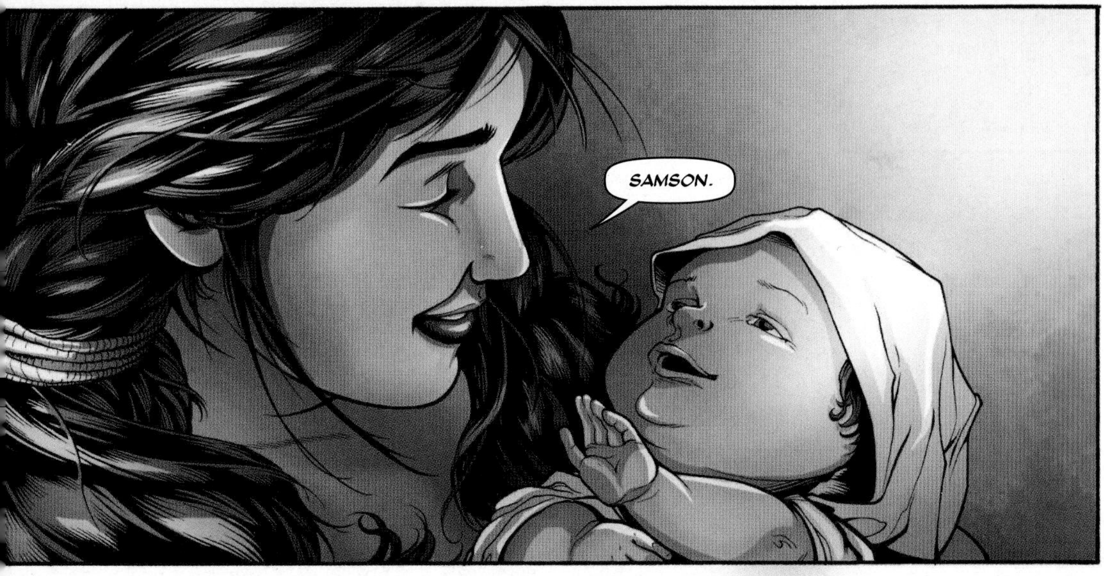
SAMSON.

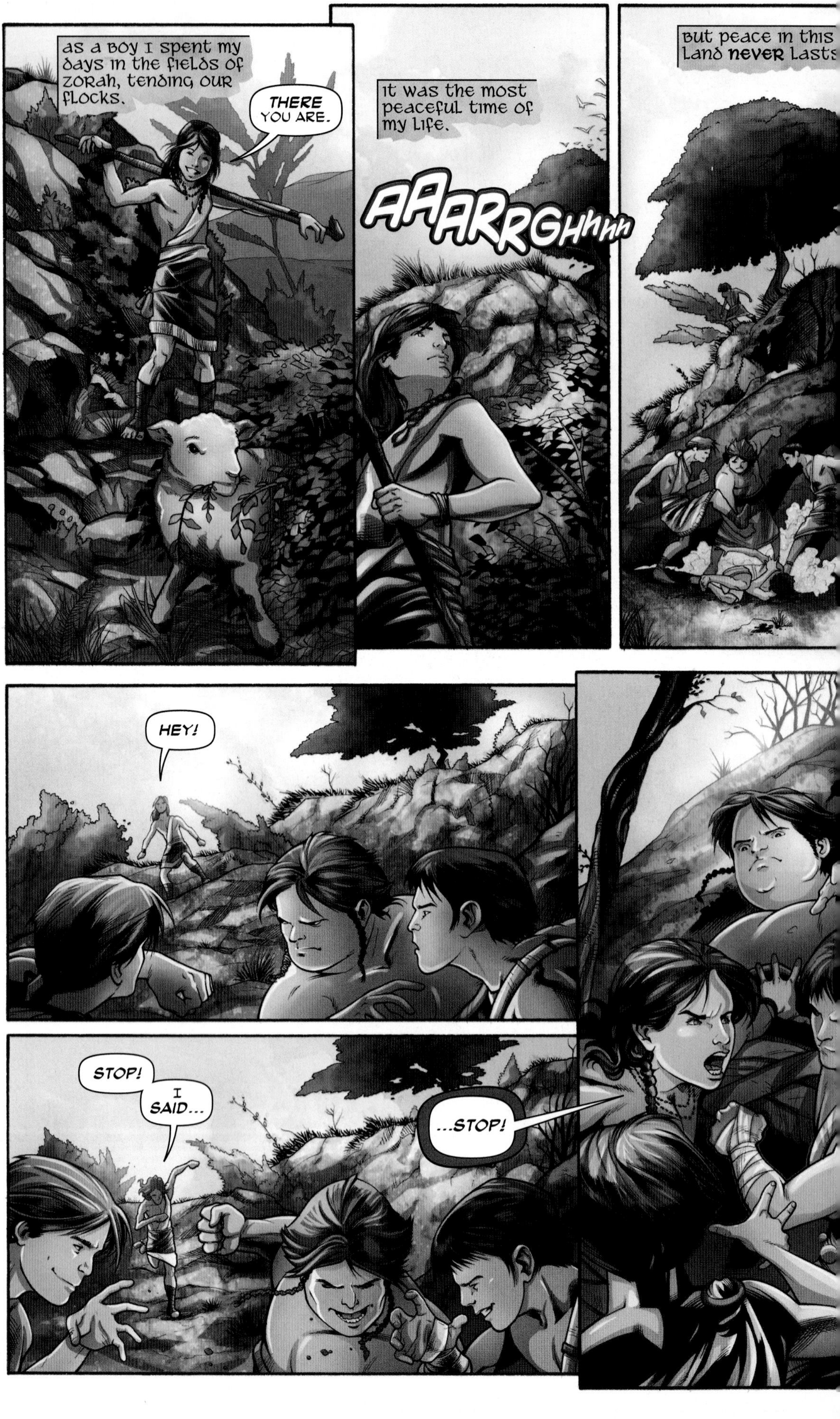
as a boy I spent my days in the fields of Zorah, tending our flocks.
THERE YOU ARE.
it was the most peaceful time of my life.
AAARRGHhhh
But peace in this land **never** lasts
HEY!
STOP!
I SAID...
...STOP!

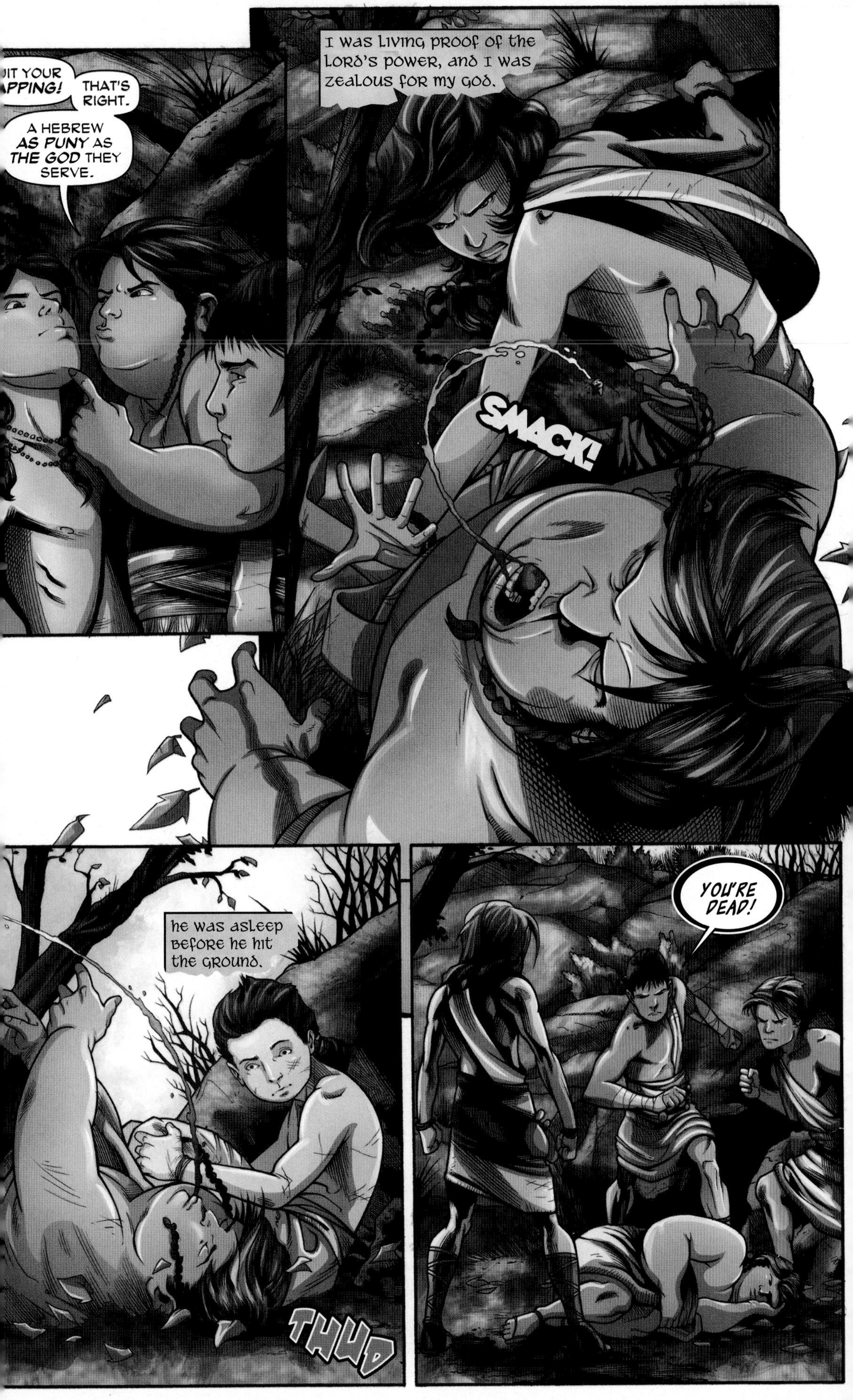

UIT YOUR
APPING!
THAT'S RIGHT.
A HEBREW AS PUNY AS THE GOD THEY SERVE.
I was living proof of the Lord's power, and I was zealous for my God.
SMACK!
he was asleep before he hit the ground.
THUD
YOU'RE DEAD!

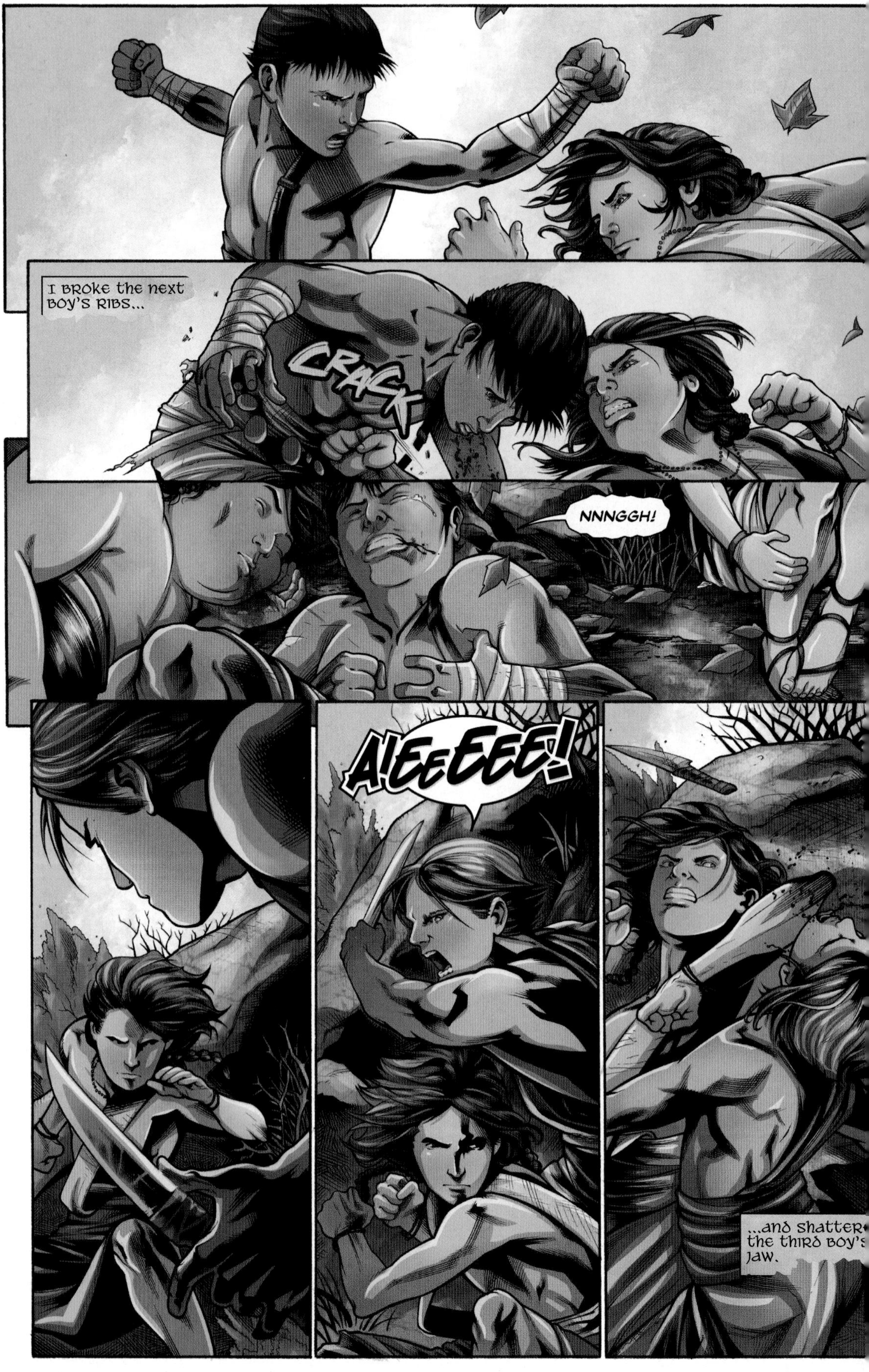

I BROKE the next BOY'S RIBS...
CRACK
NNNGGH!
AIEEEEE!
...and shatter the third boy's jaw.

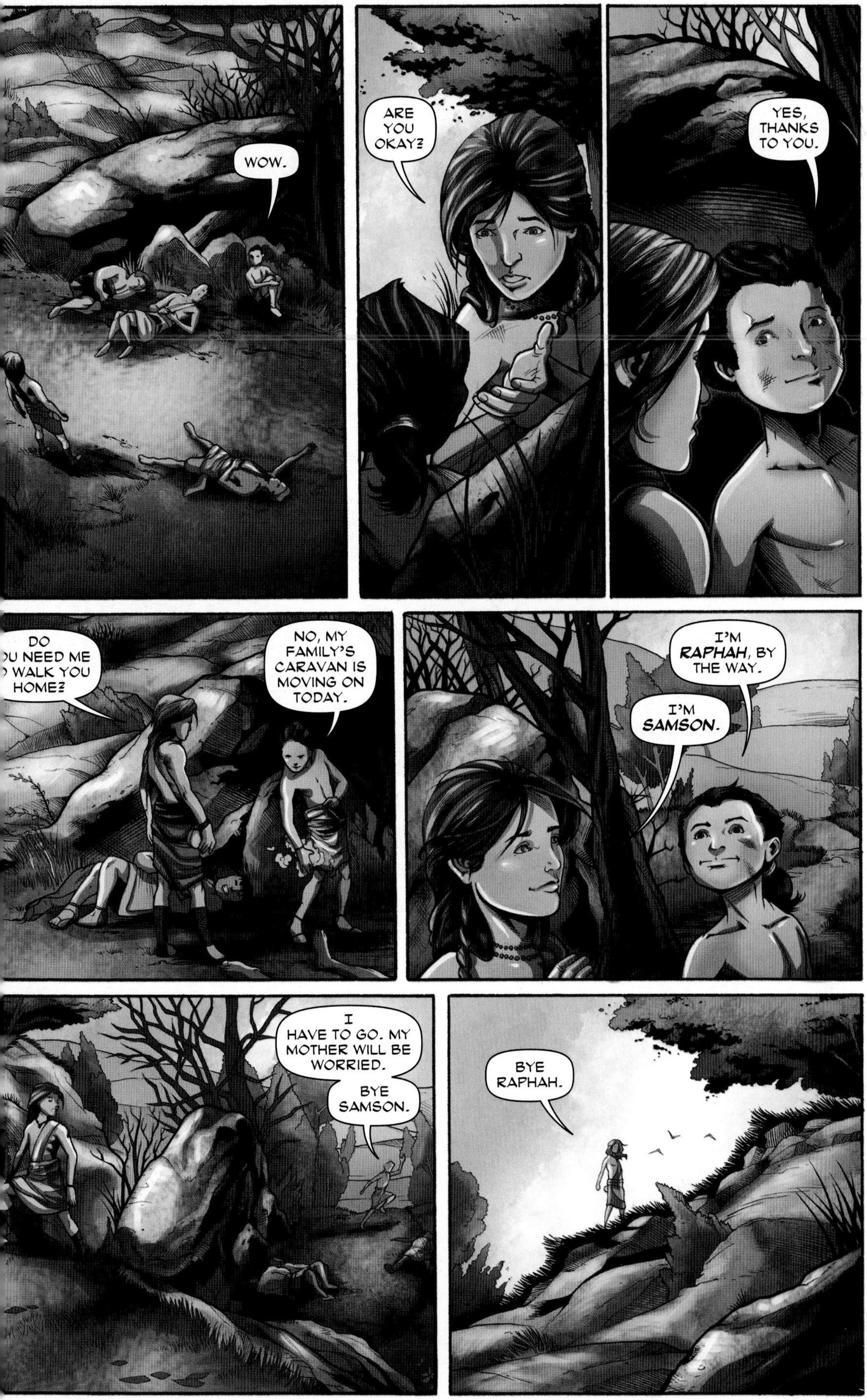
WOW.
ARE YOU OKAY?
YES, THANKS TO YOU.
DO OU NEED ME O WALK YOU HOME?
NO, MY FAMILY'S CARAVAN IS MOVING ON TODAY.
I'M RAPHAH, BY THE WAY.
I'M SAMSON.
I HAVE TO GO. MY MOTHER WILL BE WORRIED.
BYE SAMSON.
BYE RAPHAH.

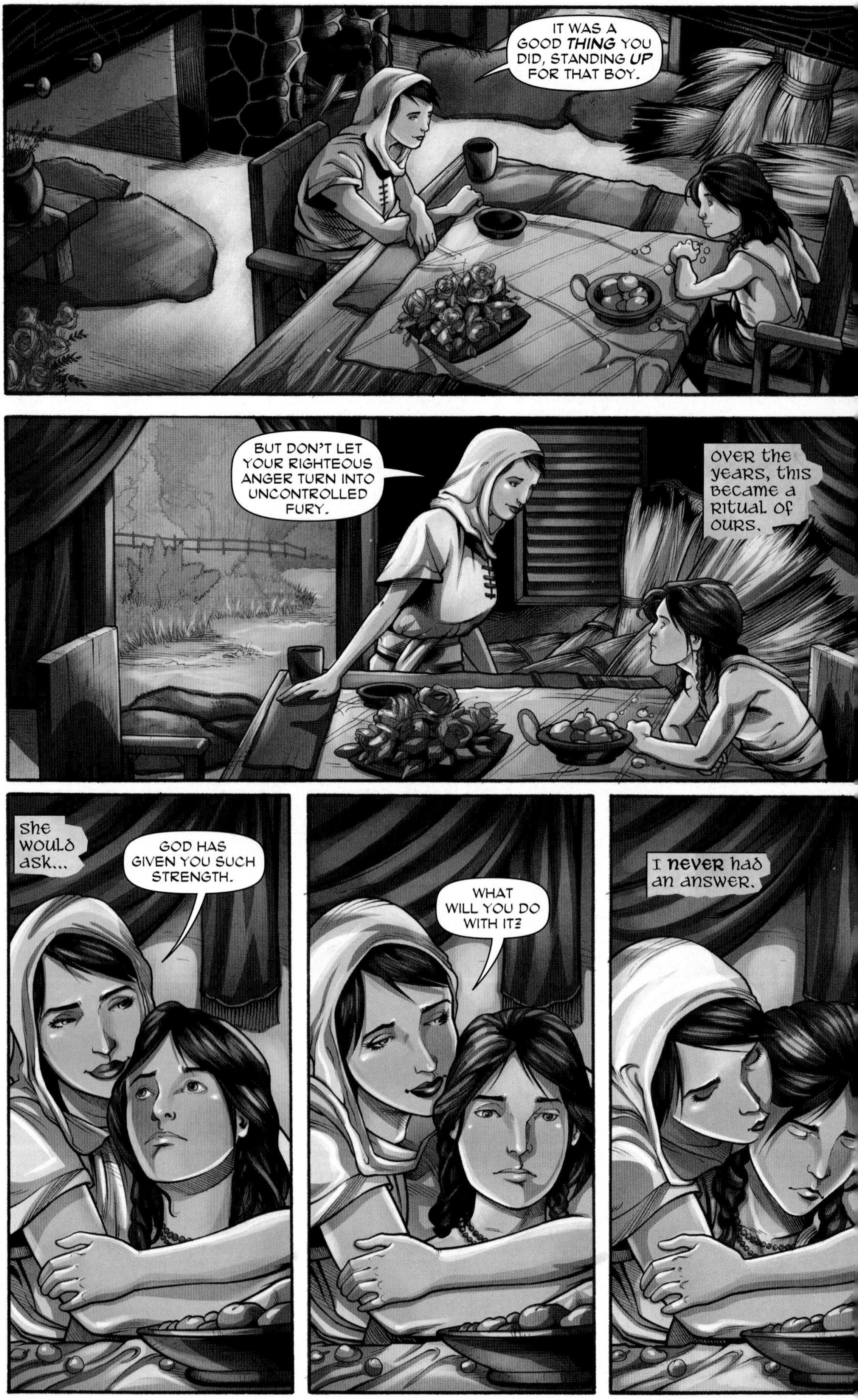
IT WAS A GOOD THING YOU DID, STANDING UP FOR THAT BOY.
BUT DON'T LET YOUR RIGHTEOUS ANGER TURN INTO UNCONTROLLED FURY.
Over the years, this became a ritual of ours.
She would ask...
GOD HAS GIVEN YOU SUCH STRENGTH.
WHAT WILL YOU DO WITH IT?
I never had an answer.

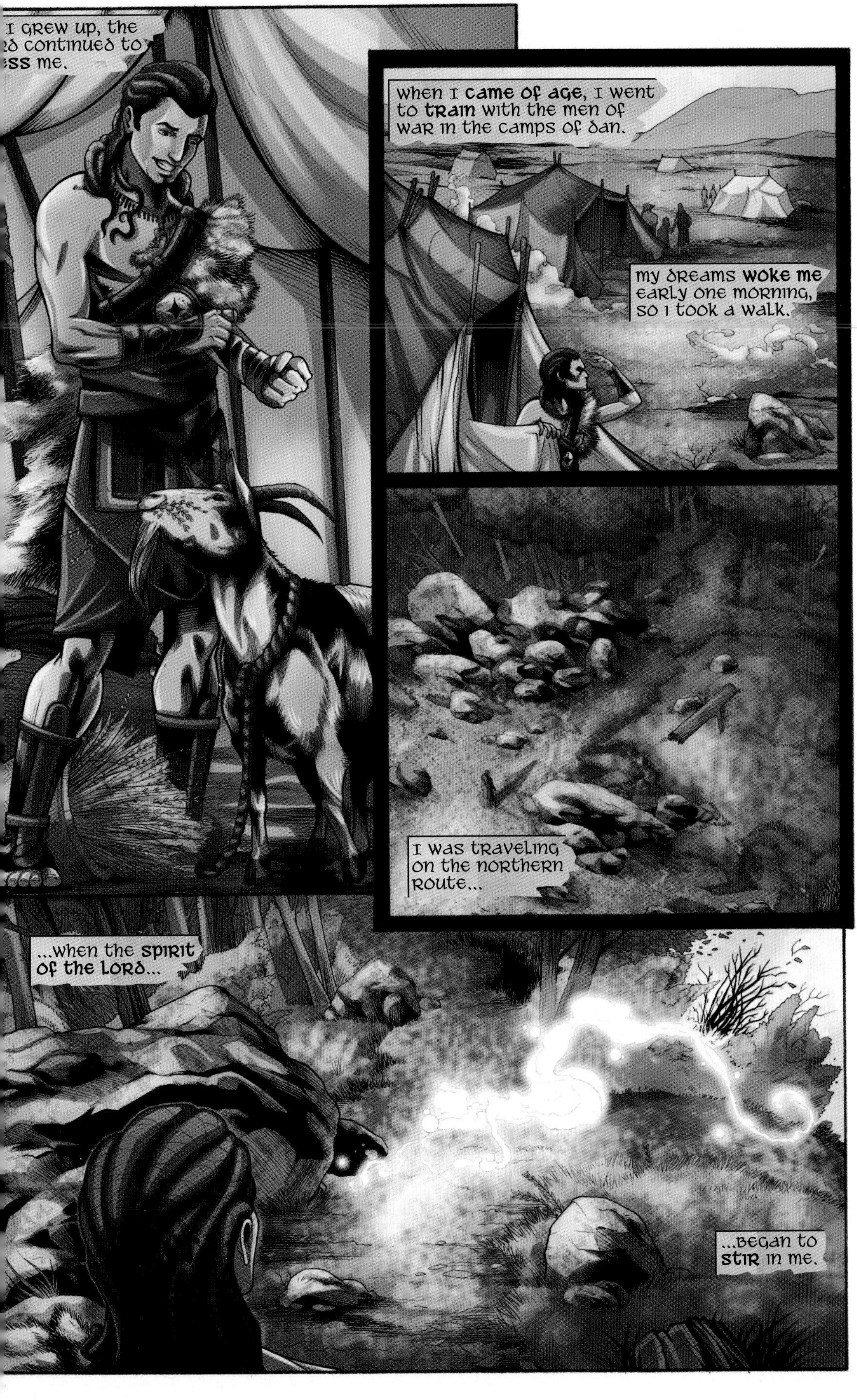
I GREW UP, THE
RD CONTINUED TO
SS ME.
WHEN I CAME OF AGE, I WENT TO TRAIN WITH THE MEN OF WAR IN THE CAMPS OF DAN.
MY DREAMS WOKE ME EARLY ONE MORNING, SO I TOOK A WALK.
I WAS TRAVELING ON THE NORTHERN ROUTE...
...WHEN THE SPIRIT OF THE LORD...
...BEGAN TO STIR IN ME.

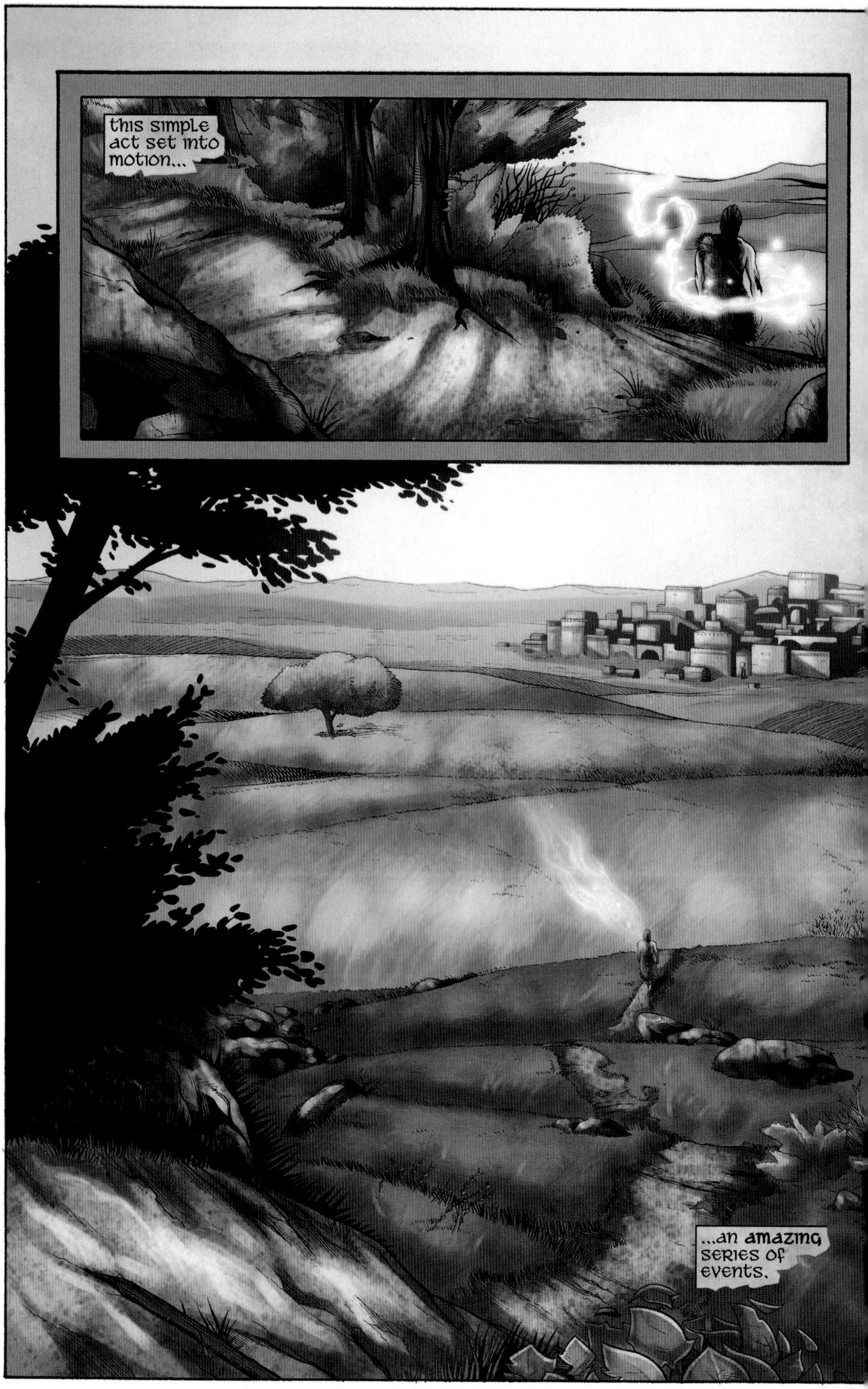

this simple act set into motion...
...an amazing series of events.

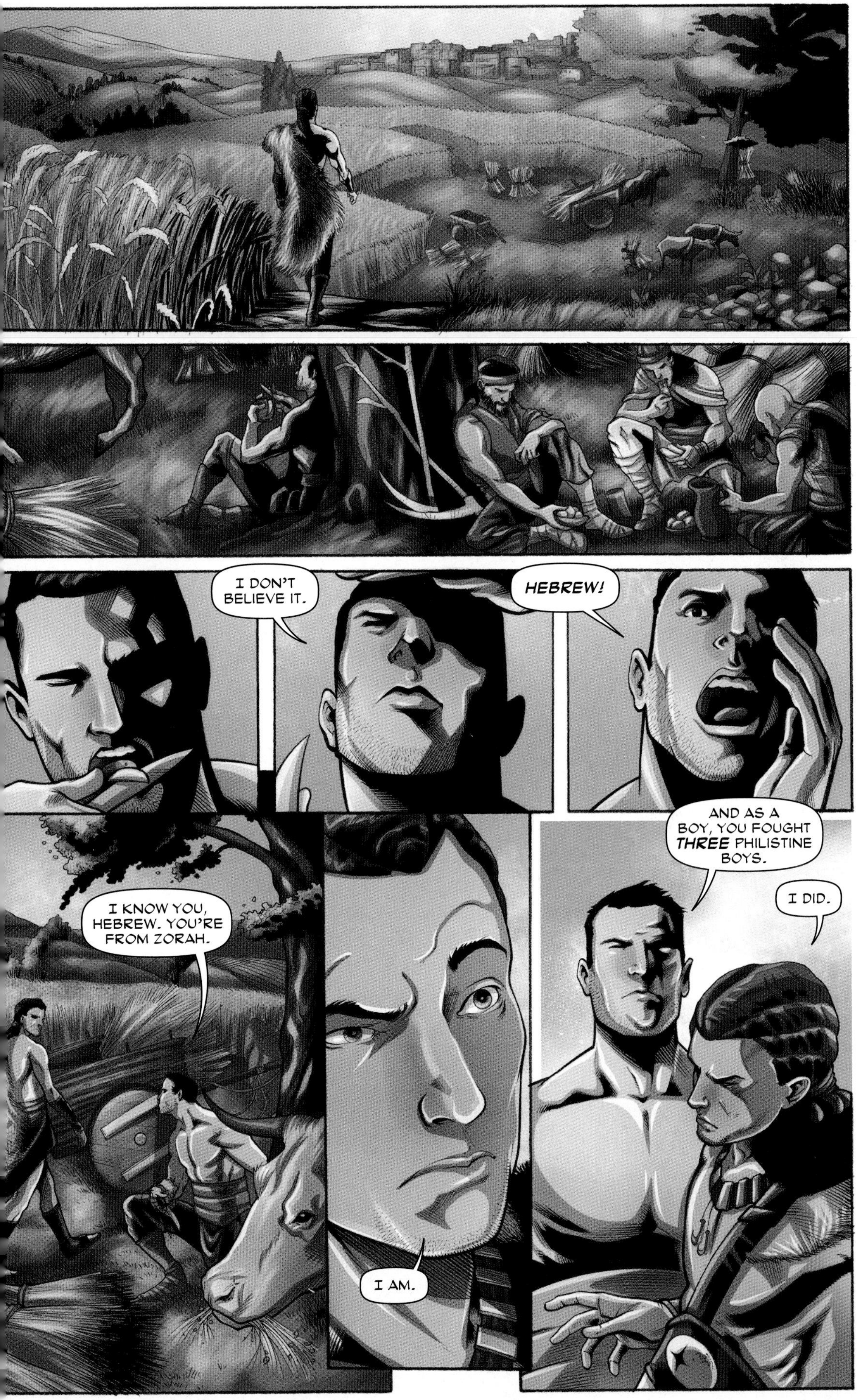

I DON'T BELIEVE IT.
HEBREW!
I KNOW YOU, HEBREW. YOU'RE FROM ZORAH.
I AM.
AND AS A BOY, YOU FOUGHT THREE PHILISTINE BOYS.
I DID.

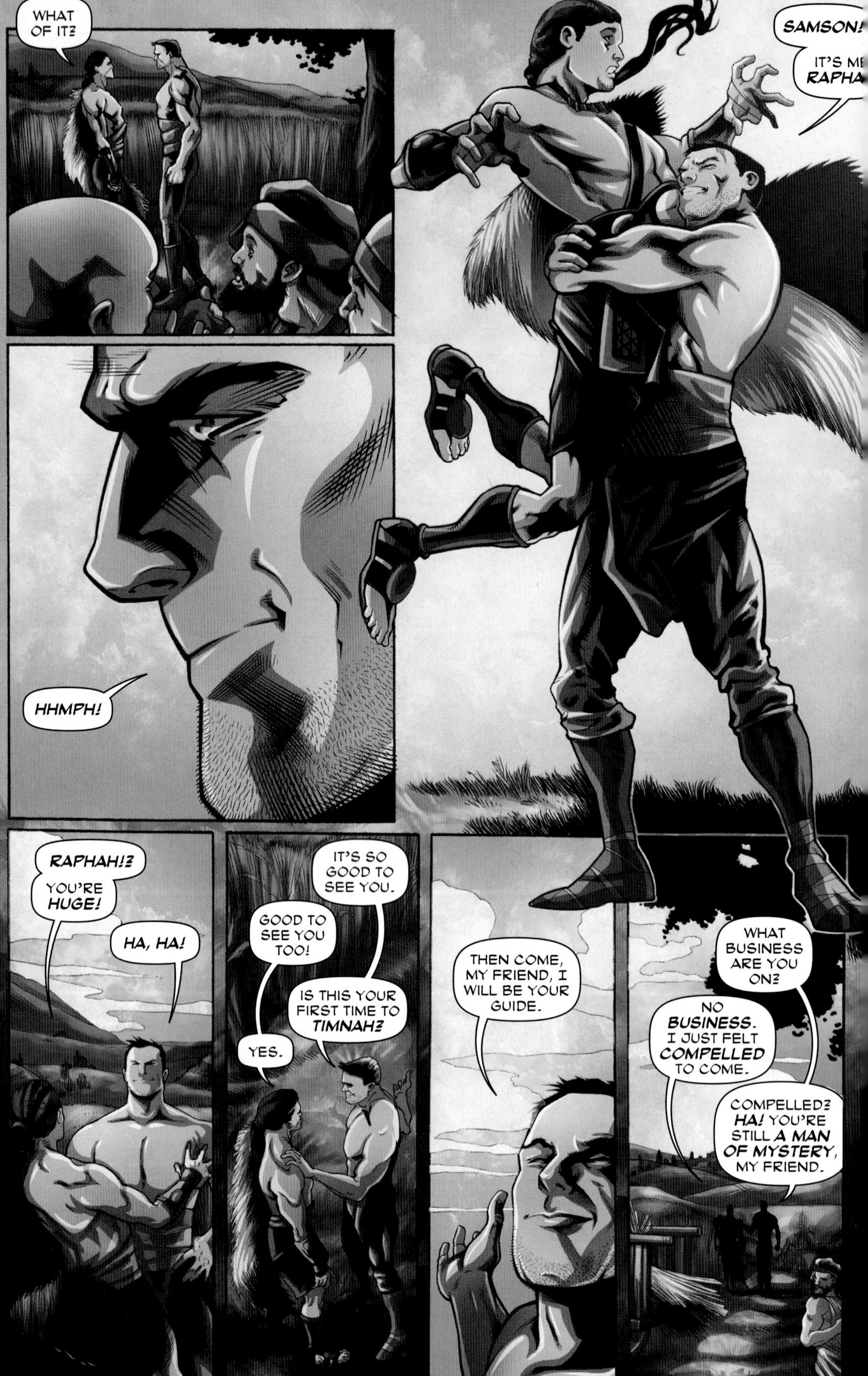

WHAT OF IT?
HHMPH!
SAMSON!
IT'S ME RAPHA
RAPHAH!?
YOU'RE HUGE!
HA, HA!
IT'S SO GOOD TO SEE YOU.
GOOD TO SEE YOU TOO!
IS THIS YOUR FIRST TIME TO TIMNAH?
YES.
THEN COME, MY FRIEND, I WILL BE YOUR GUIDE.
WHAT BUSINESS ARE YOU ON?
NO BUSINESS. I JUST FELT COMPELLED TO COME.
COMPELLED? HA! YOU'RE STILL A MAN OF MYSTERY, MY FRIEND.

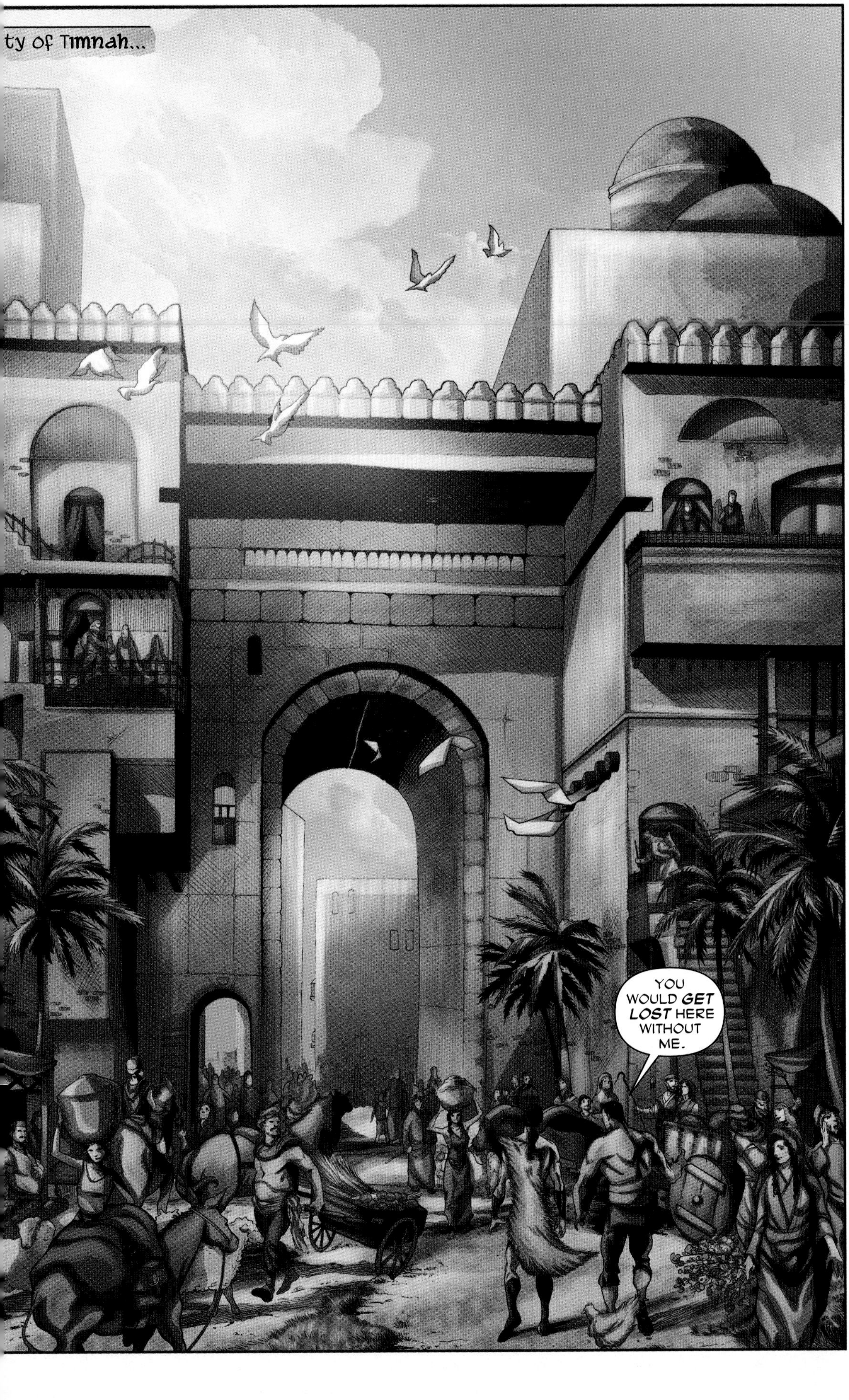
ty of Timnah...
YOU WOULD GET LOST HERE WITHOUT ME.

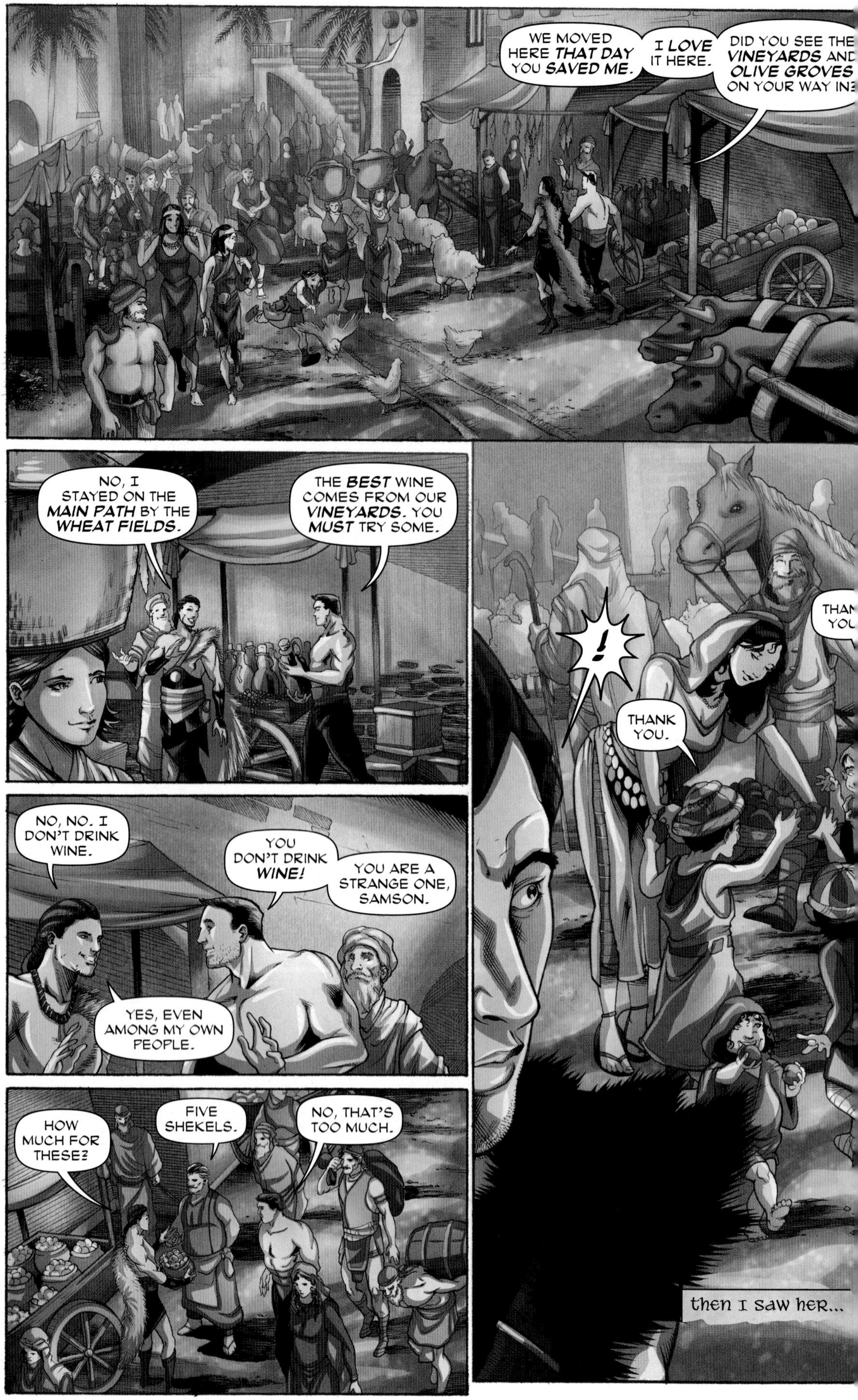
WE MOVED HERE THAT DAY YOU SAVED ME.
I LOVE IT HERE.
DID YOU SEE THE VINEYARDS AND OLIVE GROVES ON YOUR WAY IN?
NO, I STAYED ON THE MAIN PATH BY THE WHEAT FIELDS.
THE BEST WINE COMES FROM OUR VINEYARDS. YOU MUST TRY SOME.
NO, NO. I DON'T DRINK WINE.
YOU DON'T DRINK WINE!
YOU ARE A STRANGE ONE, SAMSON.
YES, EVEN AMONG MY OWN PEOPLE.
HOW MUCH FOR THESE?
FIVE SHEKELS.
NO, THAT'S TOO MUCH.
!
THANK YOU.
then I saw her...

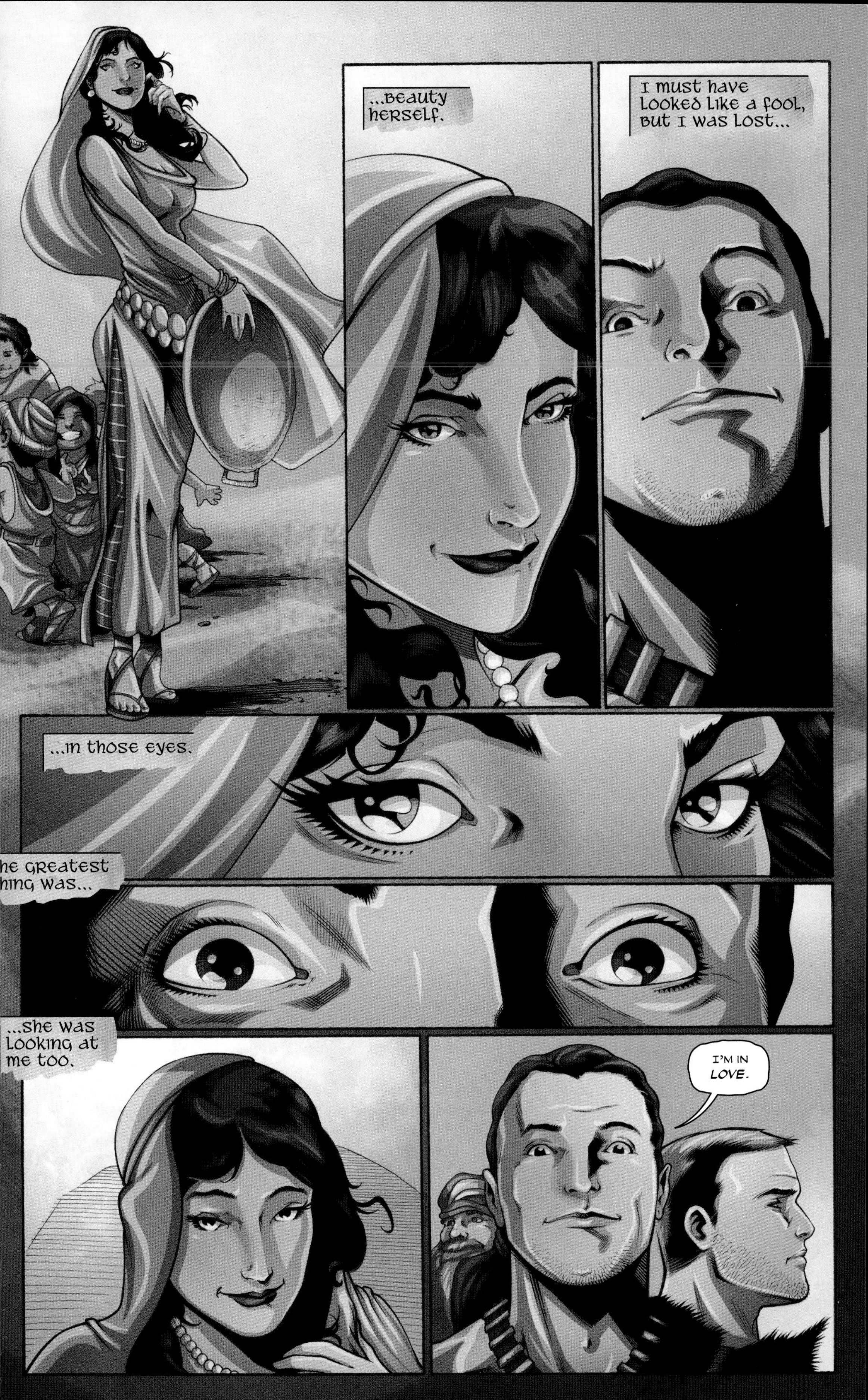
...Beauty herself.
I must have looked like a fool, but I was lost...
...in those eyes.
he greatest hing was...
...she was looking at me too.
I'M IN LOVE.

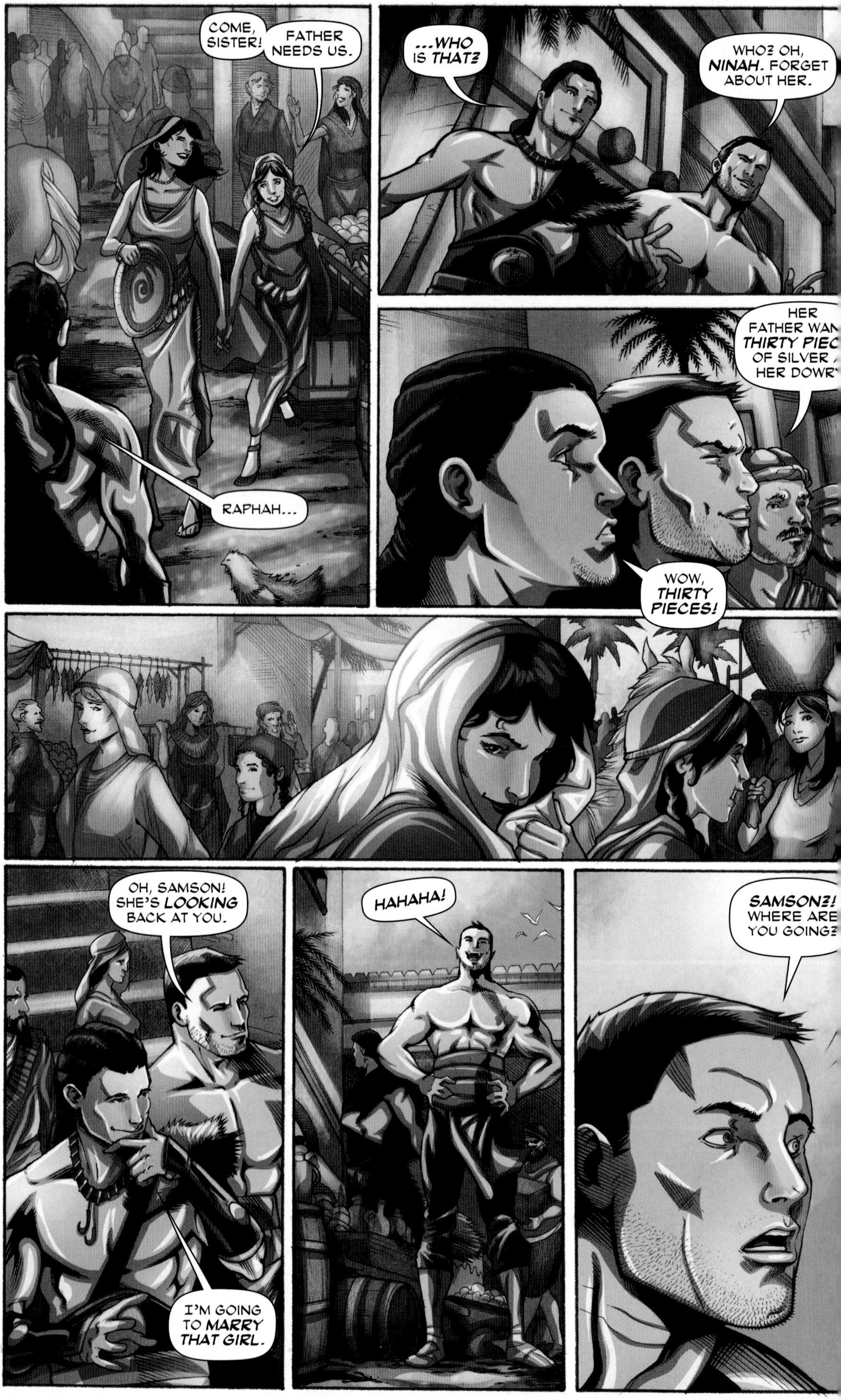
COME, SISTER!
FATHER NEEDS US.
RAPHAH...
...WHO IS THAT?
WHO? OH, NINAH. FORGET ABOUT HER.
HER FATHER WAN THIRTY PIEC OF SILVER HER DOWR
WOW, THIRTY PIECES!
OH, SAMSON! SHE'S LOOKING BACK AT YOU.
I'M GOING TO MARRY THAT GIRL.
HAHAHA!
SAMSON?! WHERE ARE YOU GOING?

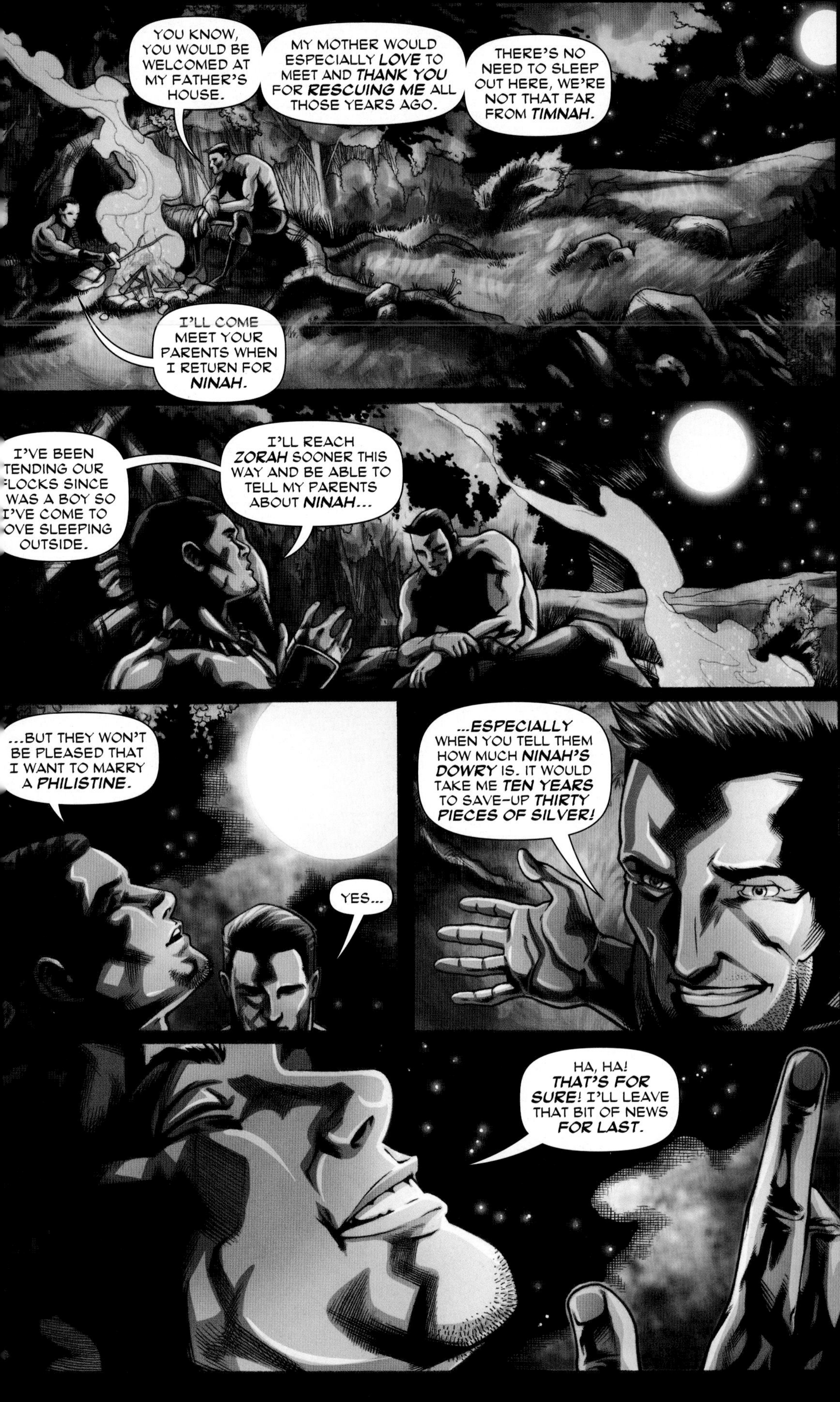
YOU KNOW, YOU WOULD BE WELCOMED AT MY FATHER'S HOUSE.
MY MOTHER WOULD ESPECIALLY LOVE TO MEET AND THANK YOU FOR RESCUING ME ALL THOSE YEARS AGO.
THERE'S NO NEED TO SLEEP OUT HERE, WE'RE NOT THAT FAR FROM TIMNAH.
I'LL COME MEET YOUR PARENTS WHEN I RETURN FOR NINAH.
I'VE BEEN TENDING OUR FLOCKS SINCE WAS A BOY SO I'VE COME TO OVE SLEEPING OUTSIDE.
I'LL REACH ZORAH SOONER THIS WAY AND BE ABLE TO TELL MY PARENTS ABOUT NINAH...
...BUT THEY WON'T BE PLEASED THAT I WANT TO MARRY A PHILISTINE.
YES...
...ESPECIALLY WHEN YOU TELL THEM HOW MUCH NINAH'S DOWRY IS. IT WOULD TAKE ME TEN YEARS TO SAVE-UP THIRTY PIECES OF SILVER!
HA, HA! THAT'S FOR SURE! I'LL LEAVE THAT BIT OF NEWS FOR LAST.

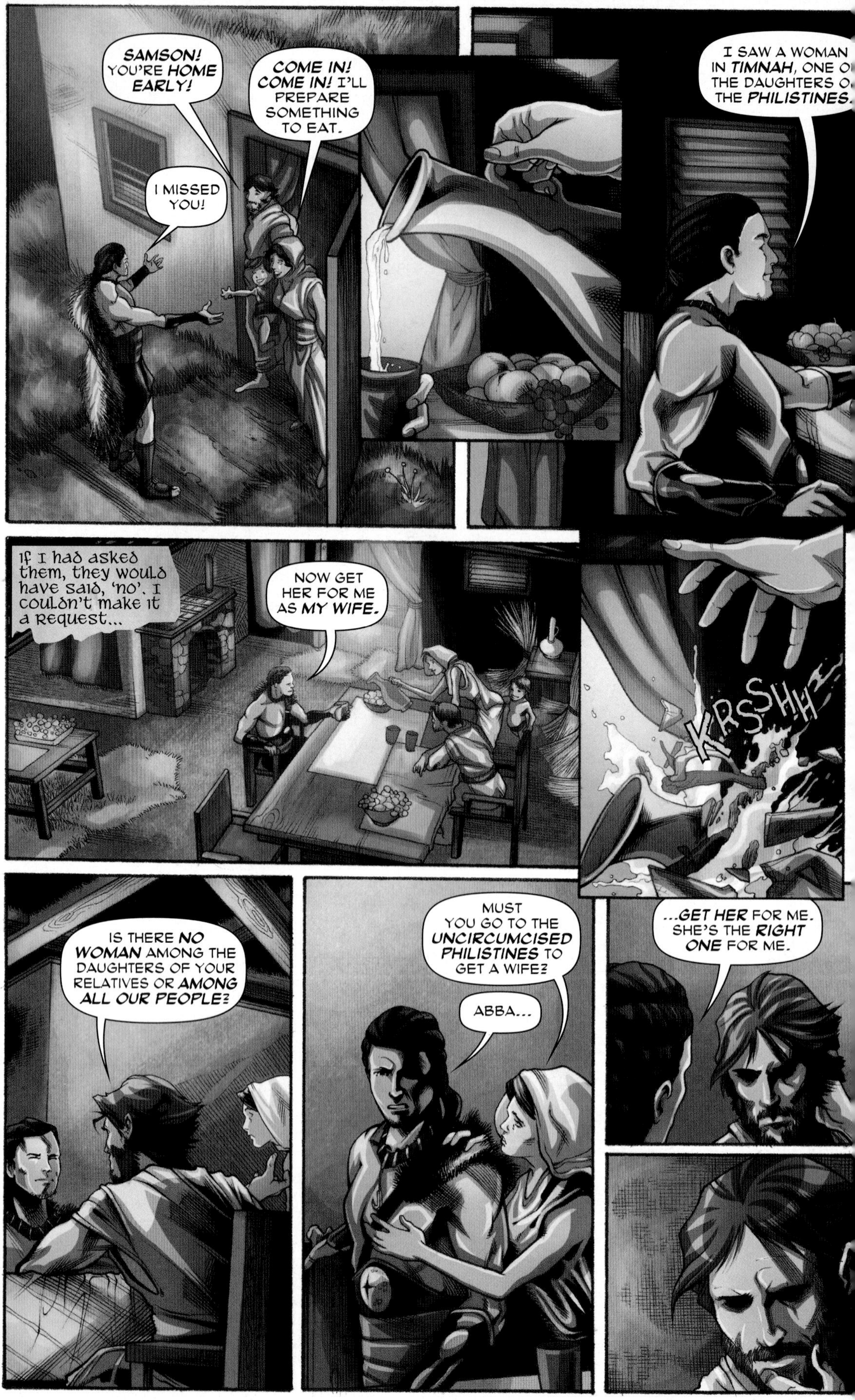
SAMSON! YOU'RE HOME EARLY!
I MISSED YOU!
COME IN! COME IN! I'LL PREPARE SOMETHING TO EAT.
I SAW A WOMAN IN TIMNAH, ONE O THE DAUGHTERS O THE PHILISTINES.
If I had asked them, they would have said, 'no'. I couldn't make it a request...
NOW GET HER FOR ME AS MY WIFE.
KRSSHH
IS THERE NO WOMAN AMONG THE DAUGHTERS OF YOUR RELATIVES OR AMONG ALL OUR PEOPLE?
MUST YOU GO TO THE UNCIRCUMCISED PHILISTINES TO GET A WIFE?
ABBA...
...GET HER FOR ME. SHE'S THE RIGHT ONE FOR ME.

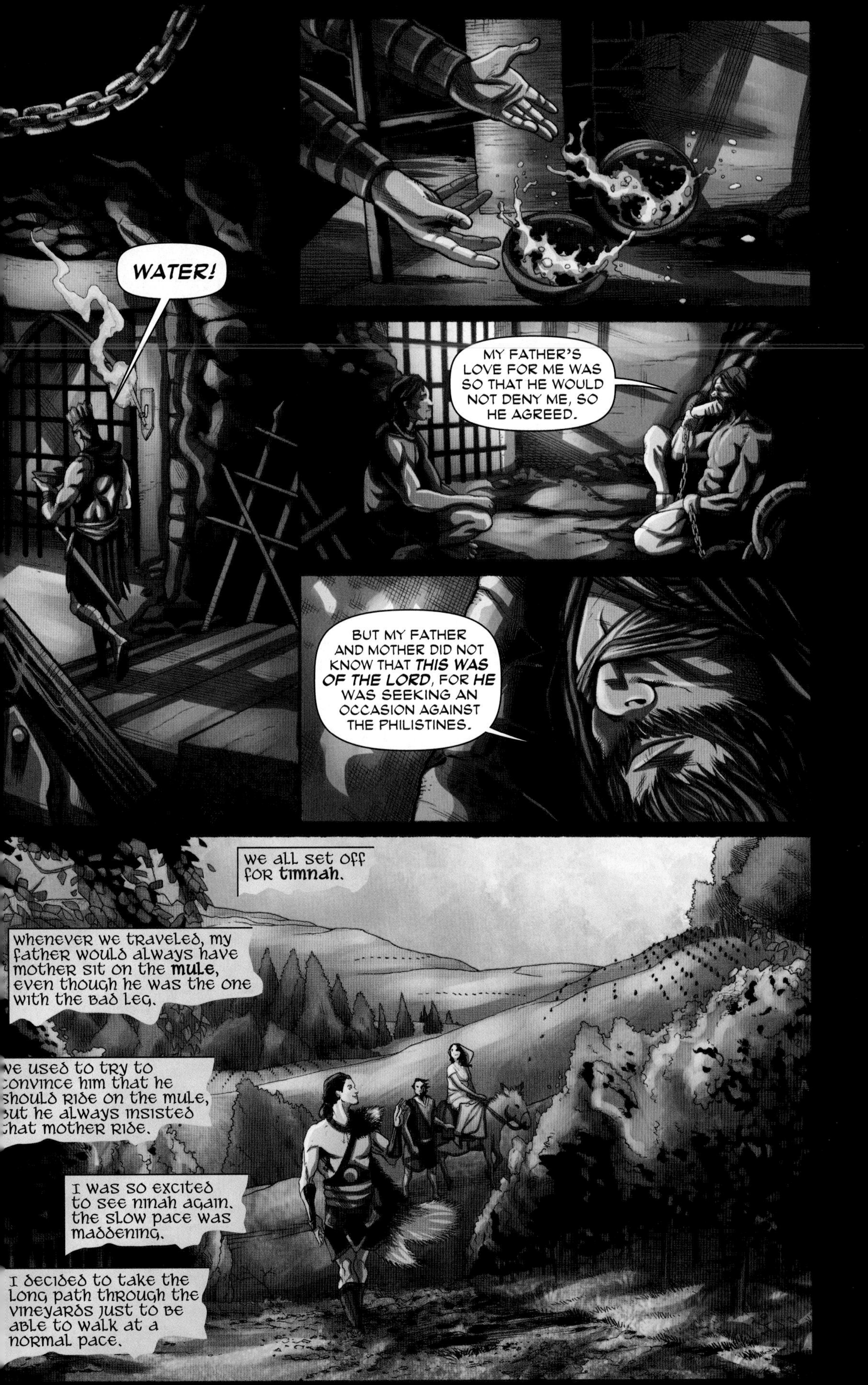

WATER!
MY FATHER'S LOVE FOR ME WAS SO THAT HE WOULD NOT DENY ME, SO HE AGREED.
BUT MY FATHER AND MOTHER DID NOT KNOW THAT *THIS WAS OF THE LORD*, FOR *HE* WAS SEEKING AN OCCASION AGAINST THE PHILISTINES.
we all set off for **timnah**.
whenever we traveled, my father would always have mother sit on the **mule**, even though he was the one with the bad leg.
ve used to try to onvince him that he should ride on the mule, ut he always insisted hat mother ride.
I was so excited to see ninah again. the slow pace was maddening.
I decided to take the long path through the vineyards just to be able to walk at a normal pace.

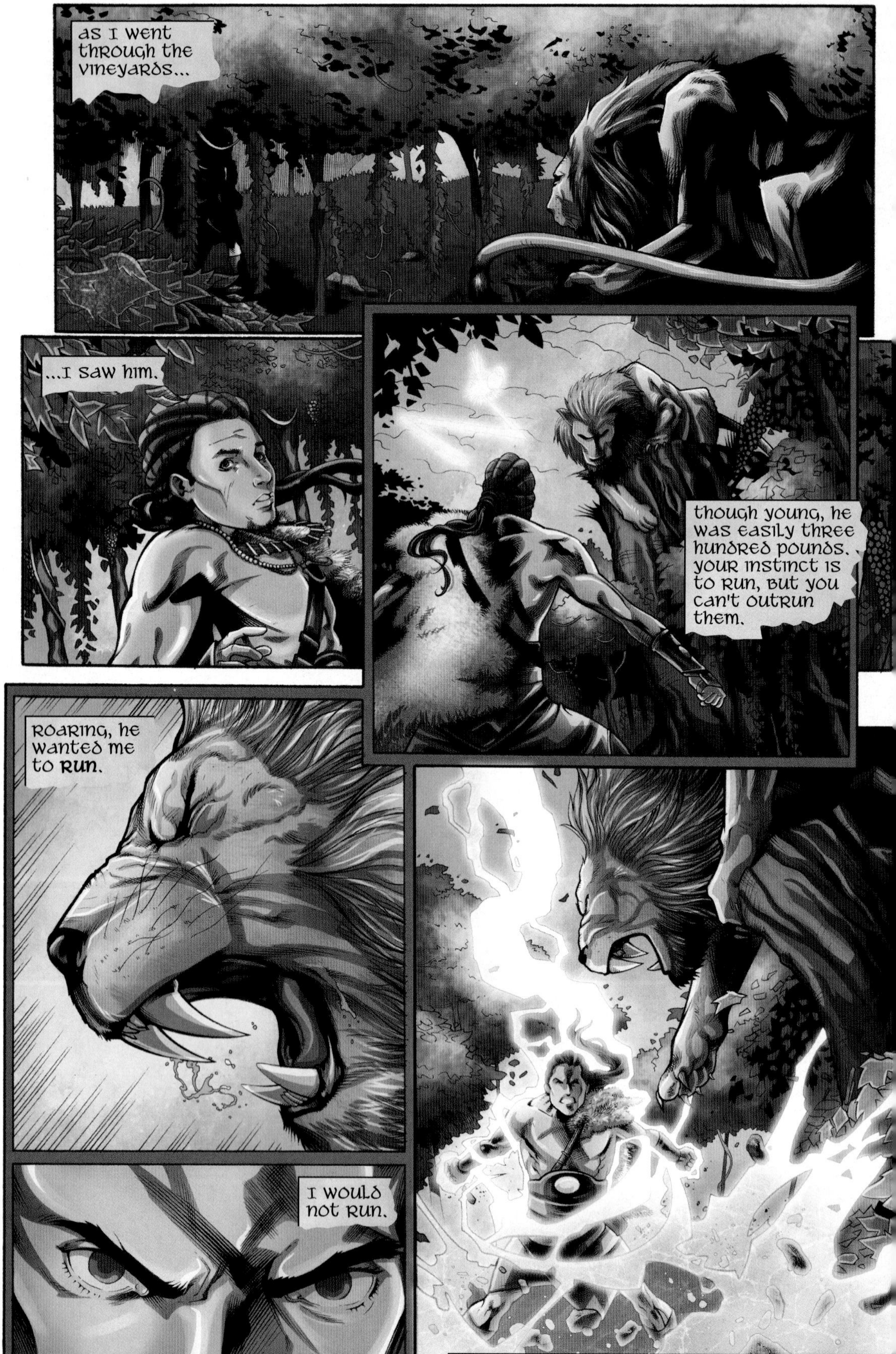
as I went through the vineyards...
...I saw him.
though young, he was easily three hundred pounds. your instinct is to run, but you can't outrun them.
Roaring, he wanted me to **run**.
I would not run.
the spirit of the lord came upon me in **power**

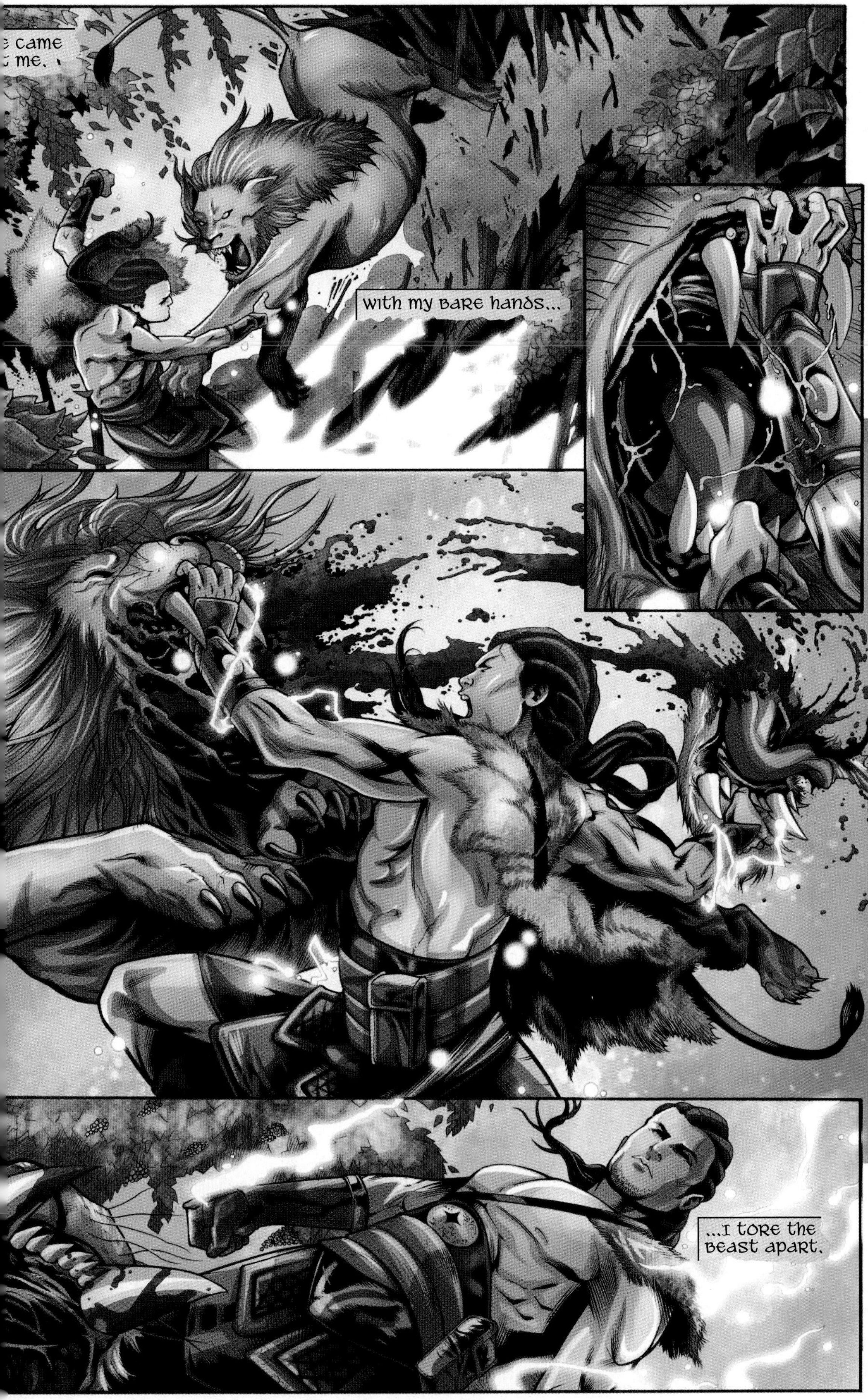
came
me.
with my bare hands...
...I tore the beast apart.

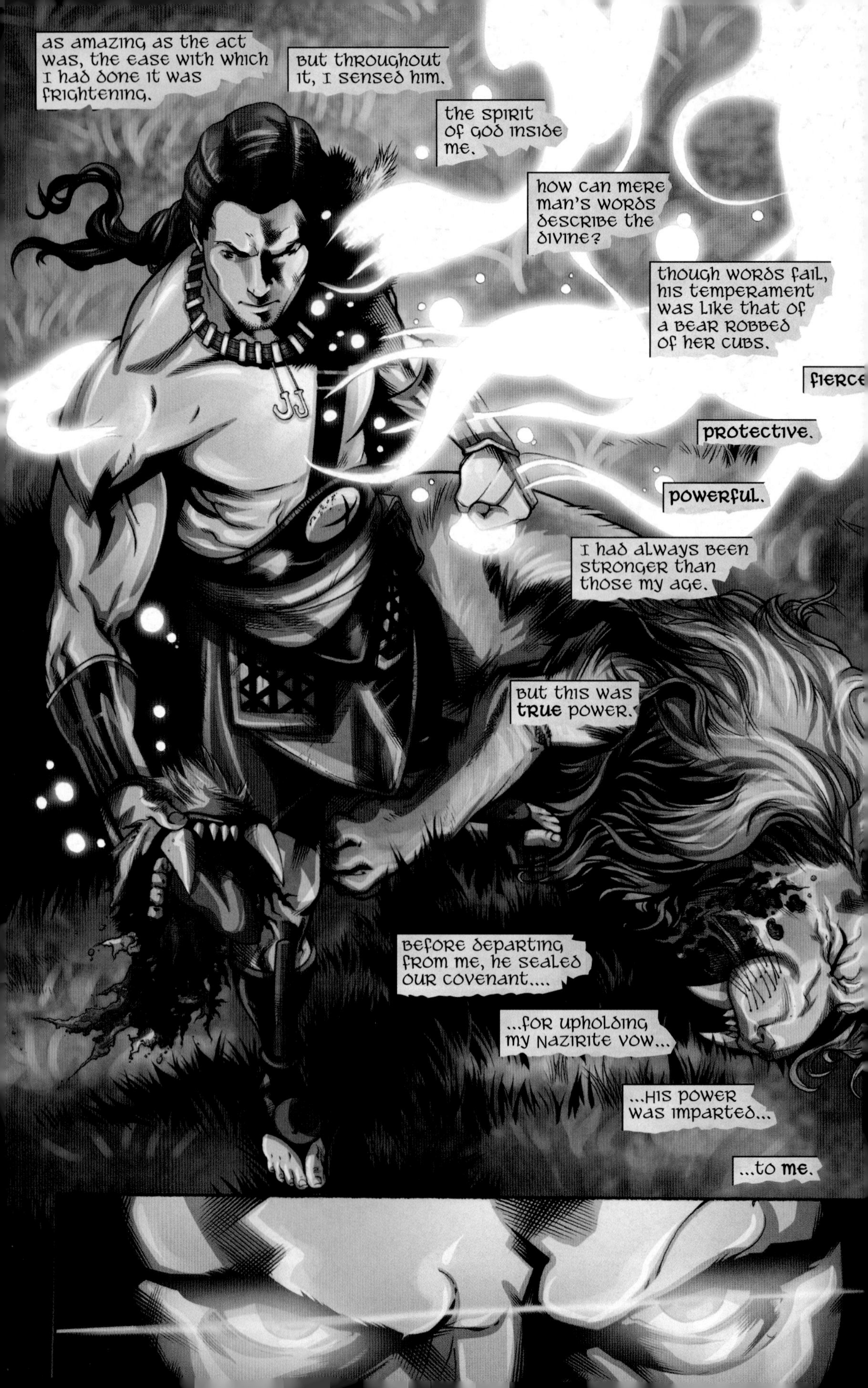
as amazing as the act was, the ease with which I had done it was frightening.
But throughout it, I sensed him.
the spirit of God inside me.
how can mere man's words describe the divine?
though words fail, his temperament was like that of a bear robbed of her cubs.
fierce.
protective.
powerful.
I had always been stronger than those my age.
But this was **true** power.
Before departing from me, he sealed our covenant....
...for upholding my Nazirite vow...
...His power was imparted...
...to **me**.

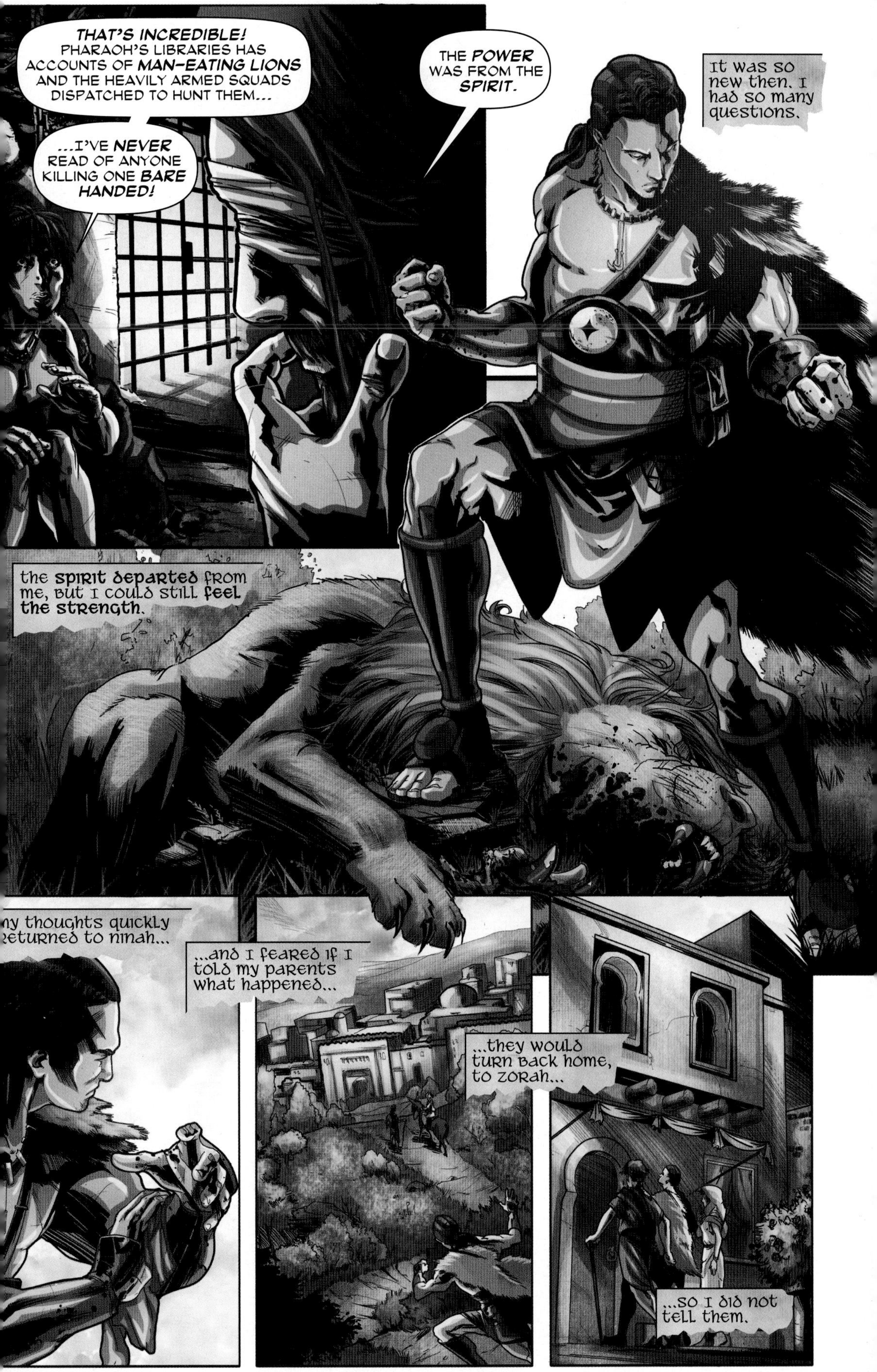
THAT'S INCREDIBLE! PHARAOH'S LIBRARIES HAS ACCOUNTS OF MAN-EATING LIONS AND THE HEAVILY ARMED SQUADS DISPATCHED TO HUNT THEM...
...I'VE NEVER READ OF ANYONE KILLING ONE BARE HANDED!
THE POWER WAS FROM THE SPIRIT.
It was so new then. I had so many questions.
the spirit departed from me, but I could still feel the strength.
my thoughts quickly returned to ninah...
...and I feared if I told my parents what happened...
...they would turn back home, to zorah...
...so I did not tell them.

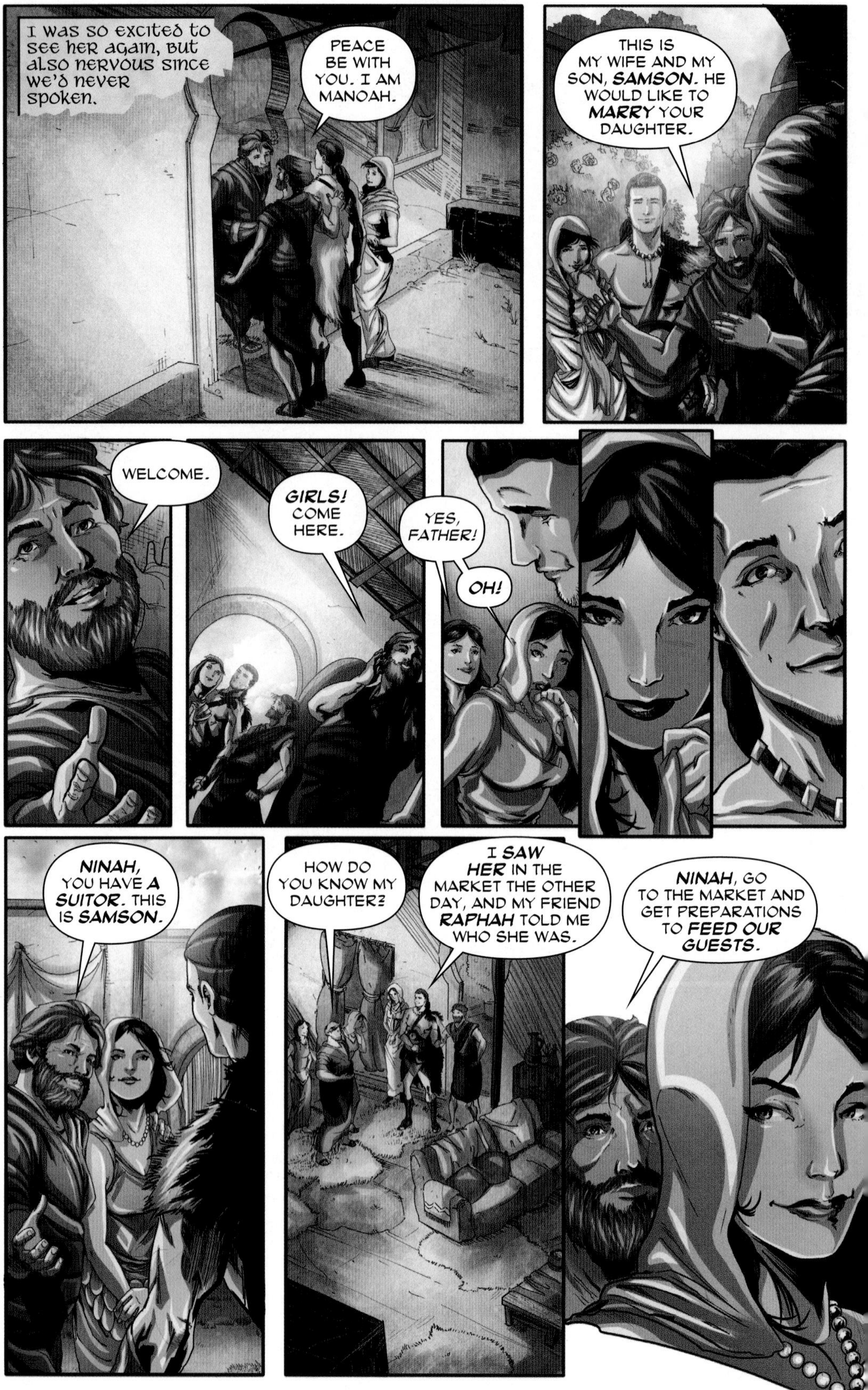

I was so excited to see her again, but also nervous since we'd never spoken.
PEACE BE WITH YOU. I AM MANOAH.
THIS IS MY WIFE AND MY SON, SAMSON. HE WOULD LIKE TO MARRY YOUR DAUGHTER.
WELCOME.
GIRLS! COME HERE.
YES, FATHER!
OH!
NINAH, YOU HAVE A SUITOR. THIS IS SAMSON.
HOW DO YOU KNOW MY DAUGHTER?
I SAW HER IN THE MARKET THE OTHER DAY, AND MY FRIEND RAPHAH TOLD ME WHO SHE WAS.
NINAH, GO TO THE MARKET AND GET PREPARATIONS TO FEED OUR GUESTS.

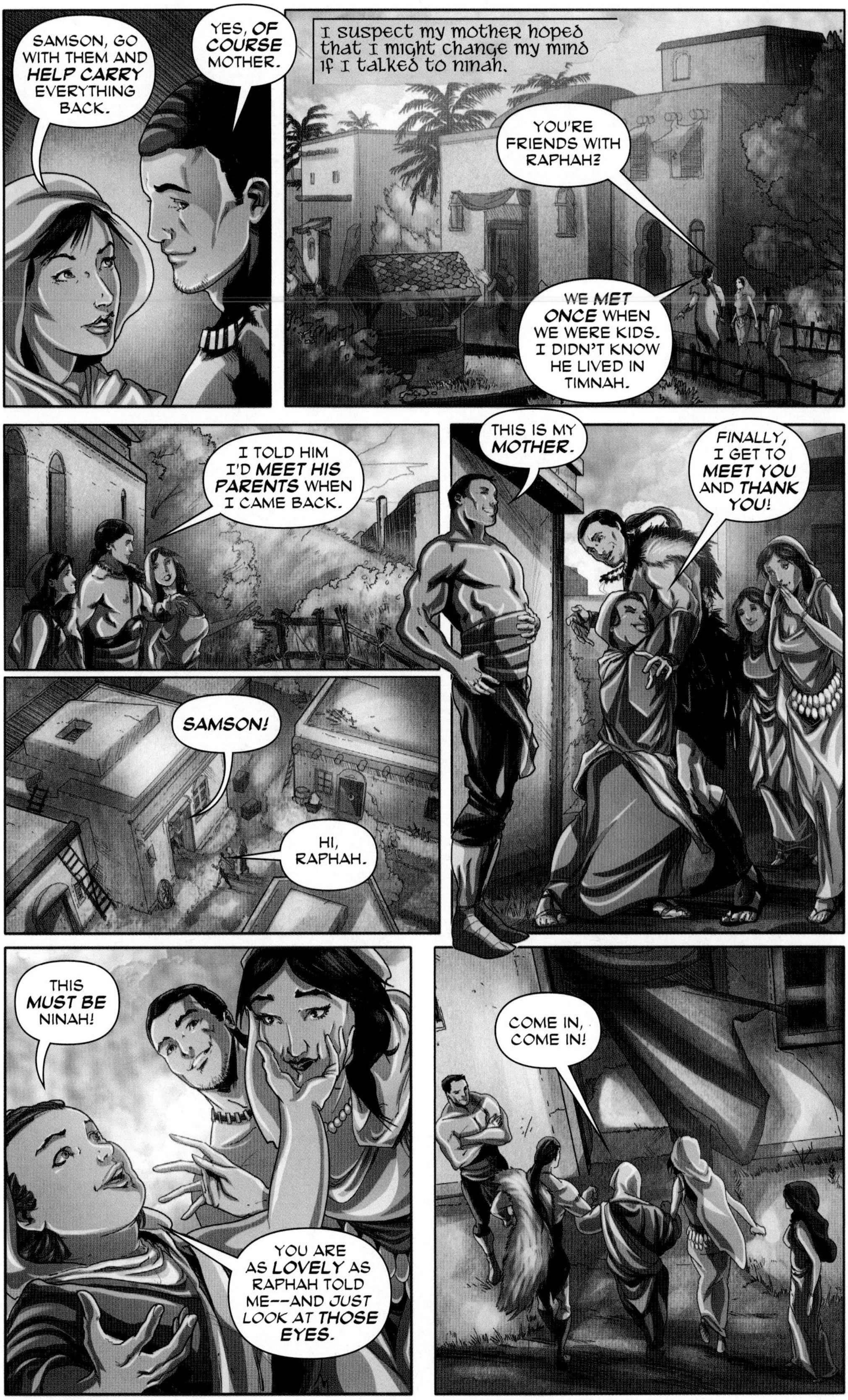
SAMSON, GO WITH THEM AND HELP CARRY EVERYTHING BACK.
YES, OF COURSE MOTHER.
I suspect my mother hoped that I might change my mind if I talked to ninah.
YOU'RE FRIENDS WITH RAPHAH?
WE MET ONCE WHEN WE WERE KIDS. I DIDN'T KNOW HE LIVED IN TIMNAH.
I TOLD HIM I'D MEET HIS PARENTS WHEN I CAME BACK.
SAMSON!
HI, RAPHAH.
THIS IS MY MOTHER.
FINALLY, I GET TO MEET YOU AND THANK YOU!
THIS MUST BE NINAH!
YOU ARE AS LOVELY AS RAPHAH TOLD ME--AND JUST LOOK AT THOSE EYES.
COME IN, COME IN!

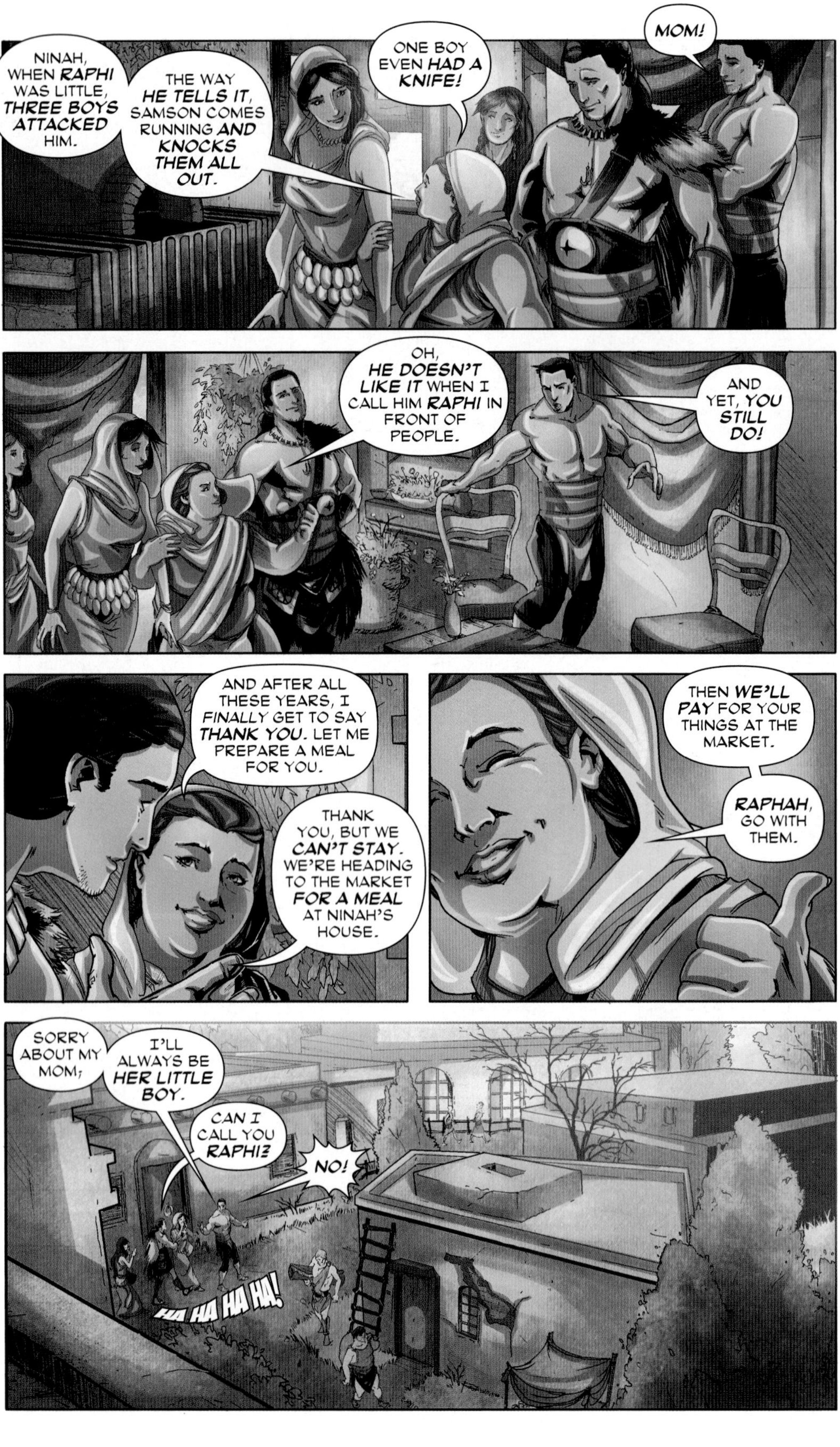
NINAH, WHEN RAPHI WAS LITTLE, THREE BOYS ATTACKED HIM.
THE WAY HE TELLS IT, SAMSON COMES RUNNING AND KNOCKS THEM ALL OUT.
ONE BOY EVEN HAD A KNIFE!
MOM!
OH, HE DOESN'T LIKE IT WHEN I CALL HIM RAPHI IN FRONT OF PEOPLE.
AND YET, YOU STILL DO!
AND AFTER ALL THESE YEARS, I FINALLY GET TO SAY THANK YOU. LET ME PREPARE A MEAL FOR YOU.
THANK YOU, BUT WE CAN'T STAY. WE'RE HEADING TO THE MARKET FOR A MEAL AT NINAH'S HOUSE.
THEN WE'LL PAY FOR YOUR THINGS AT THE MARKET.
RAPHAH, GO WITH THEM.
SORRY ABOUT MY MOM;
I'LL ALWAYS BE HER LITTLE BOY.
CAN I CALL YOU RAPHI?
NO!
HA HA HA HA!

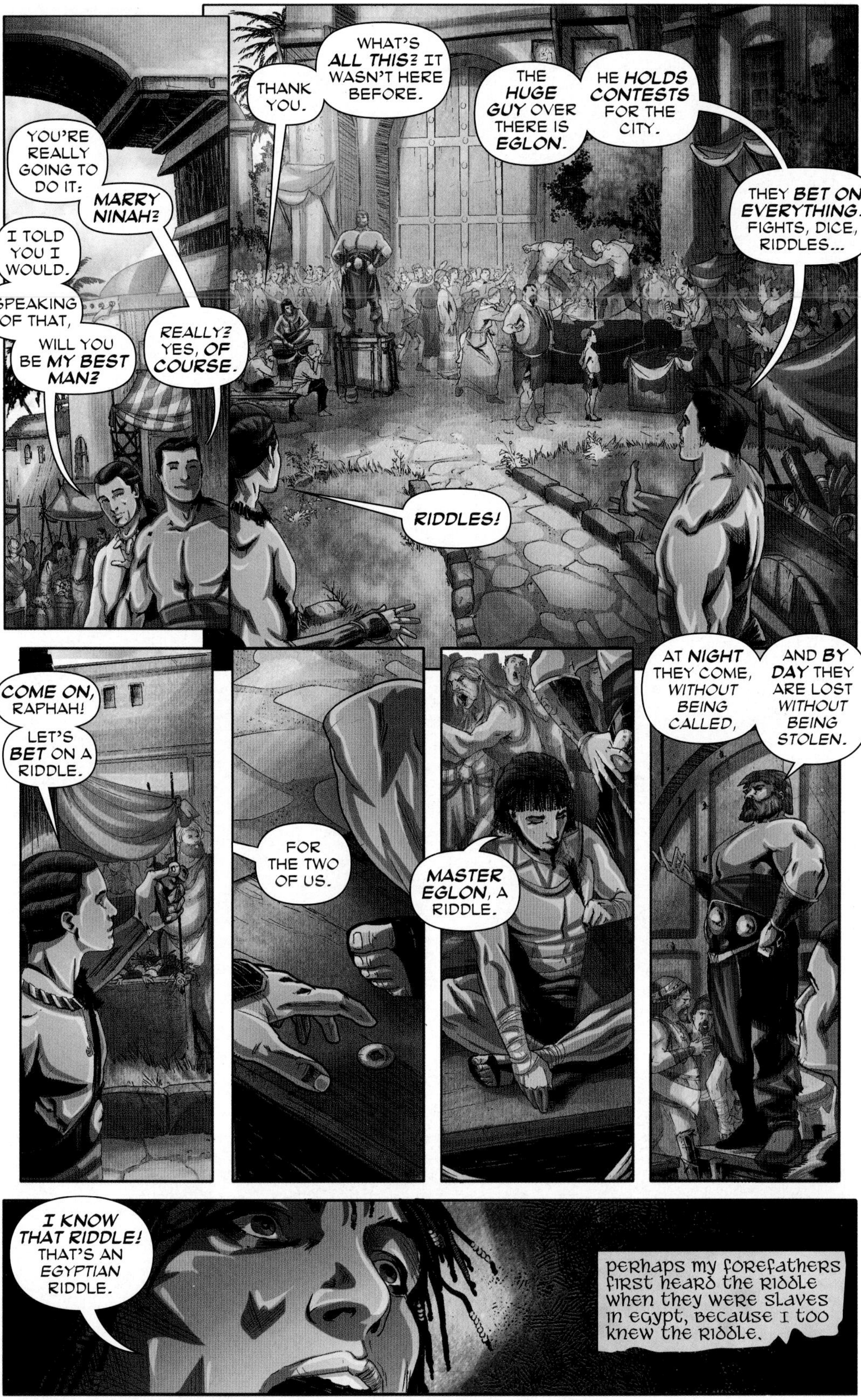

YOU'RE REALLY GOING TO DO IT: MARRY NINAH?
I TOLD YOU I WOULD.
SPEAKING OF THAT,
WILL YOU BE MY BEST MAN?
REALLY? YES, OF COURSE.
THANK YOU.
WHAT'S ALL THIS? IT WASN'T HERE BEFORE.
THE HUGE GUY OVER THERE IS EGLON.
HE HOLDS CONTESTS FOR THE CITY.
THEY BET ON EVERYTHING. FIGHTS, DICE, RIDDLES...
RIDDLES!
COME ON, RAPHAH!
LET'S BET ON A RIDDLE.
FOR THE TWO OF US.
MASTER EGLON, A RIDDLE.
AT NIGHT THEY COME, WITHOUT BEING CALLED,
AND BY DAY THEY ARE LOST WITHOUT BEING STOLEN.
I KNOW THAT RIDDLE! THAT'S AN EGYPTIAN RIDDLE.
perhaps my forefathers first heard the riddle when they were slaves in egypt, because I too knew the riddle.

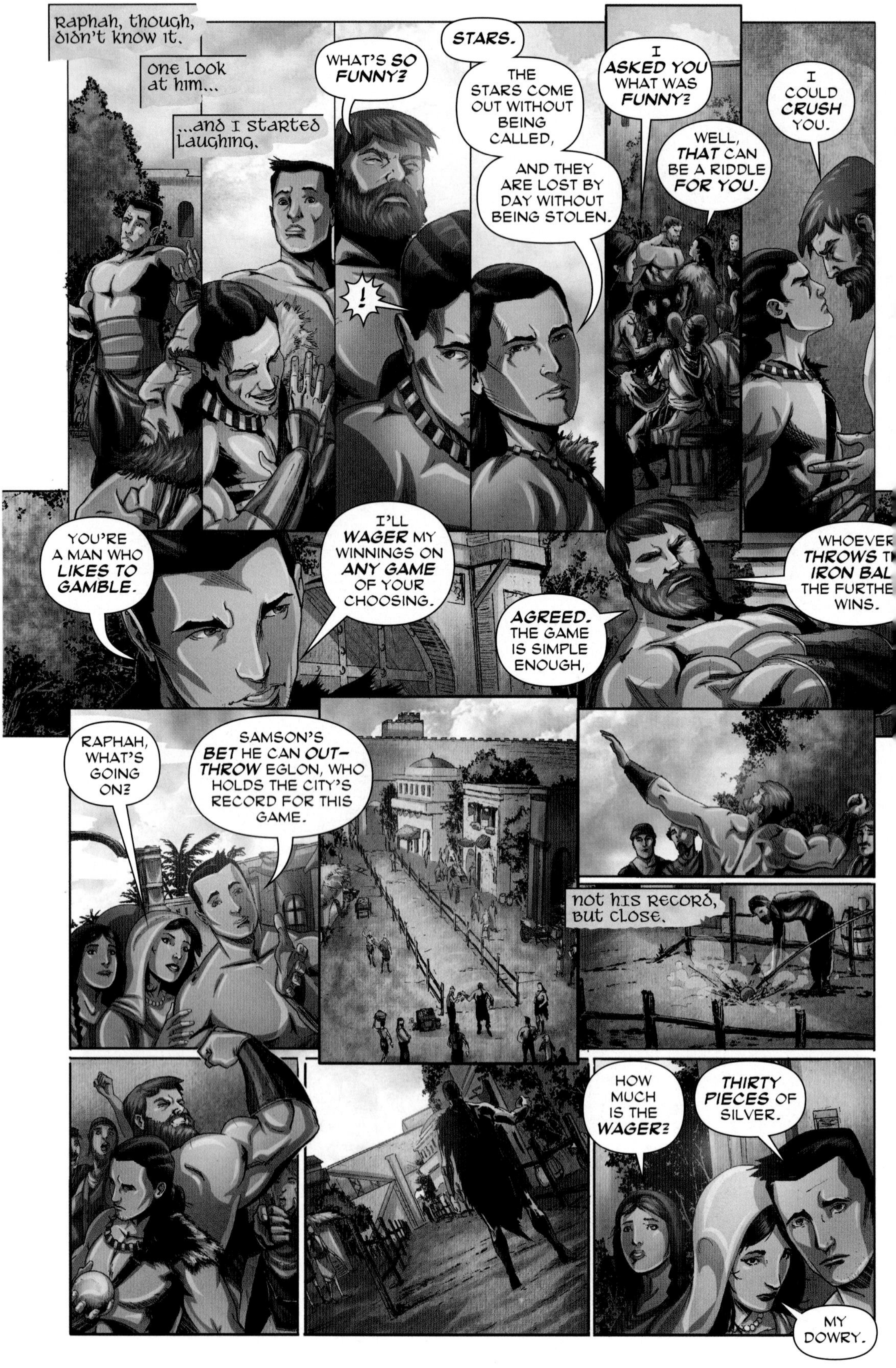
Raphah, though, didn't know it.
one look at him...
...and I started laughing.
WHAT'S SO FUNNY?
!
STARS.
THE STARS COME OUT WITHOUT BEING CALLED,
AND THEY ARE LOST BY DAY WITHOUT BEING STOLEN.
I ASKED YOU WHAT WAS FUNNY?
WELL, THAT CAN BE A RIDDLE FOR YOU.
I COULD CRUSH YOU.
YOU'RE A MAN WHO LIKES TO GAMBLE.
I'LL WAGER MY WINNINGS ON ANY GAME OF YOUR CHOOSING.
AGREED. THE GAME IS SIMPLE ENOUGH,
RAPHAH, WHAT'S GOING ON?
SAMSON'S BET HE CAN OUT-THROW EGLON, WHO HOLDS THE CITY'S RECORD FOR THIS GAME.
not his record, but close.
HOW MUCH IS THE WAGER?
THIRTY PIECES OF SILVER.
MY DOWRY.

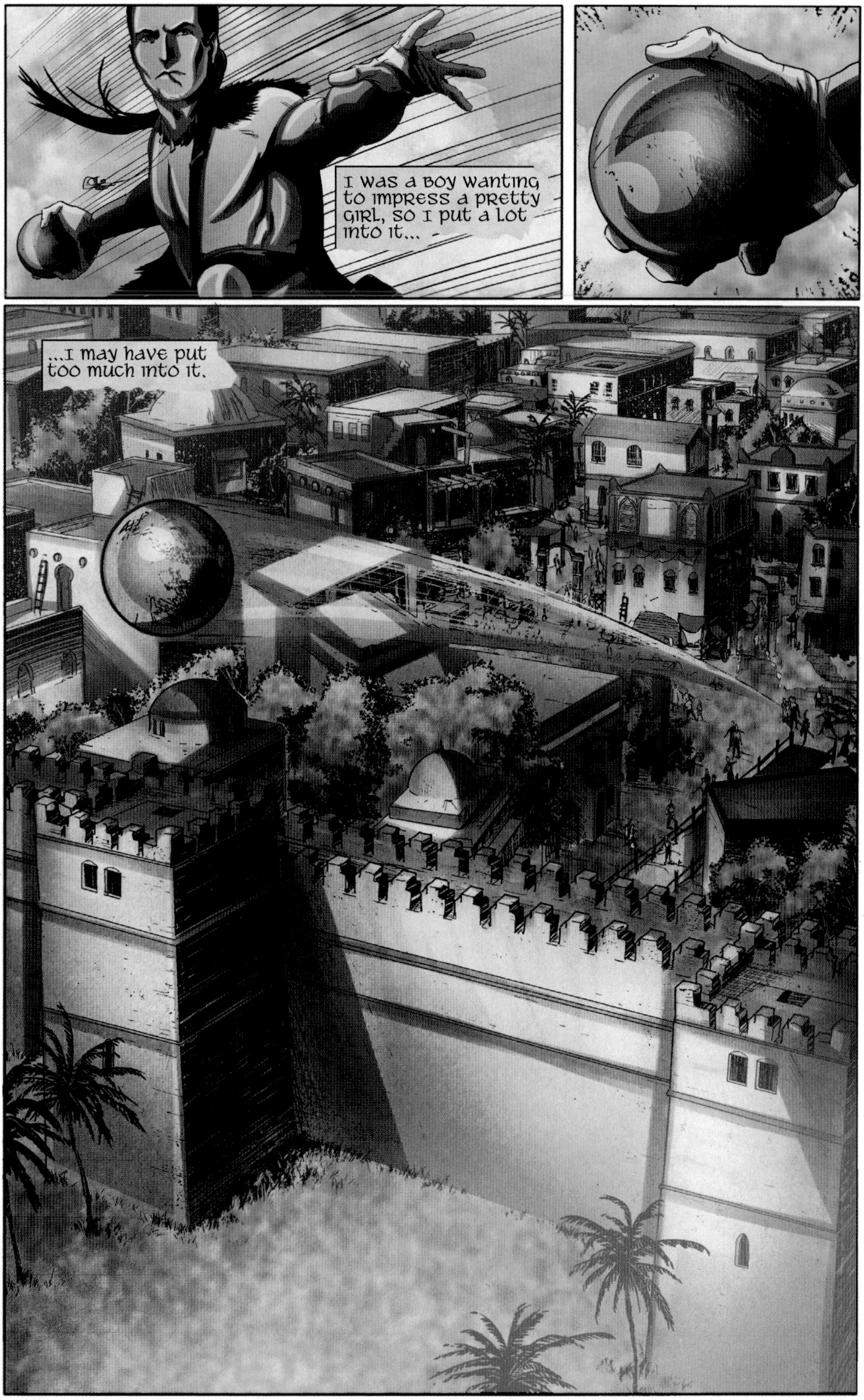
I WAS A BOY WANTING TO IMPRESS A PRETTY GIRL, SO I PUT A LOT INTO IT...
...I MAY HAVE PUT TOO MUCH INTO IT.

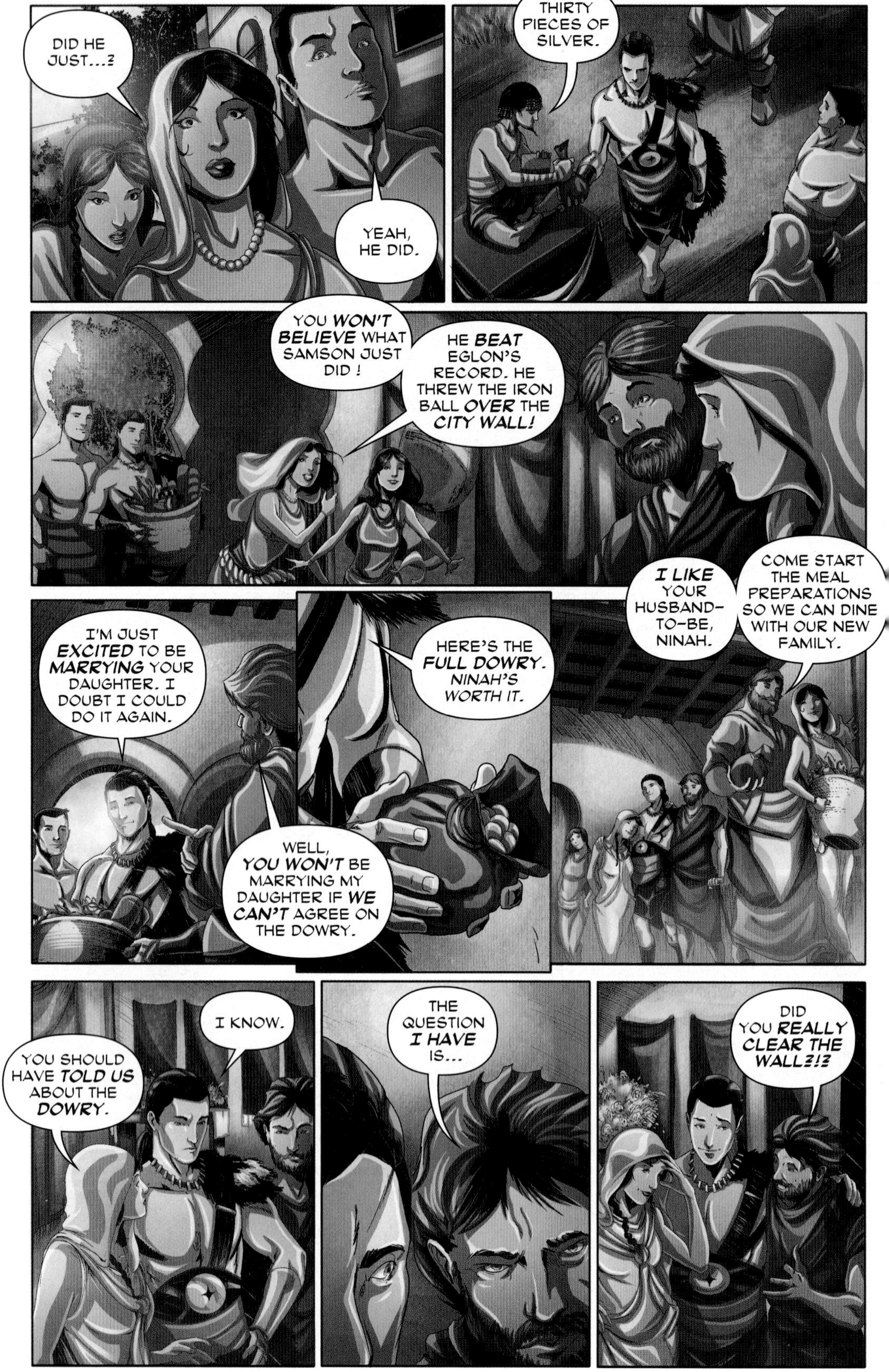
DID HE JUST...?
YEAH, HE DID.
THIRTY PIECES OF SILVER.
YOU WON'T BELIEVE WHAT SAMSON JUST DID !
HE BEAT EGLON'S RECORD. HE THREW THE IRON BALL OVER THE CITY WALL!
I LIKE YOUR HUSBAND-TO-BE, NINAH.
COME START THE MEAL PREPARATIONS SO WE CAN DINE WITH OUR NEW FAMILY.
I'M JUST EXCITED TO BE MARRYING YOUR DAUGHTER. I DOUBT I COULD DO IT AGAIN.
WELL, YOU WON'T BE MARRYING MY DAUGHTER IF WE CAN'T AGREE ON THE DOWRY.
HERE'S THE FULL DOWRY. NINAH'S WORTH IT.
YOU SHOULD HAVE TOLD US ABOUT THE DOWRY.
I KNOW.
THE QUESTION I HAVE IS...
DID YOU REALLY CLEAR THE WALL?!?

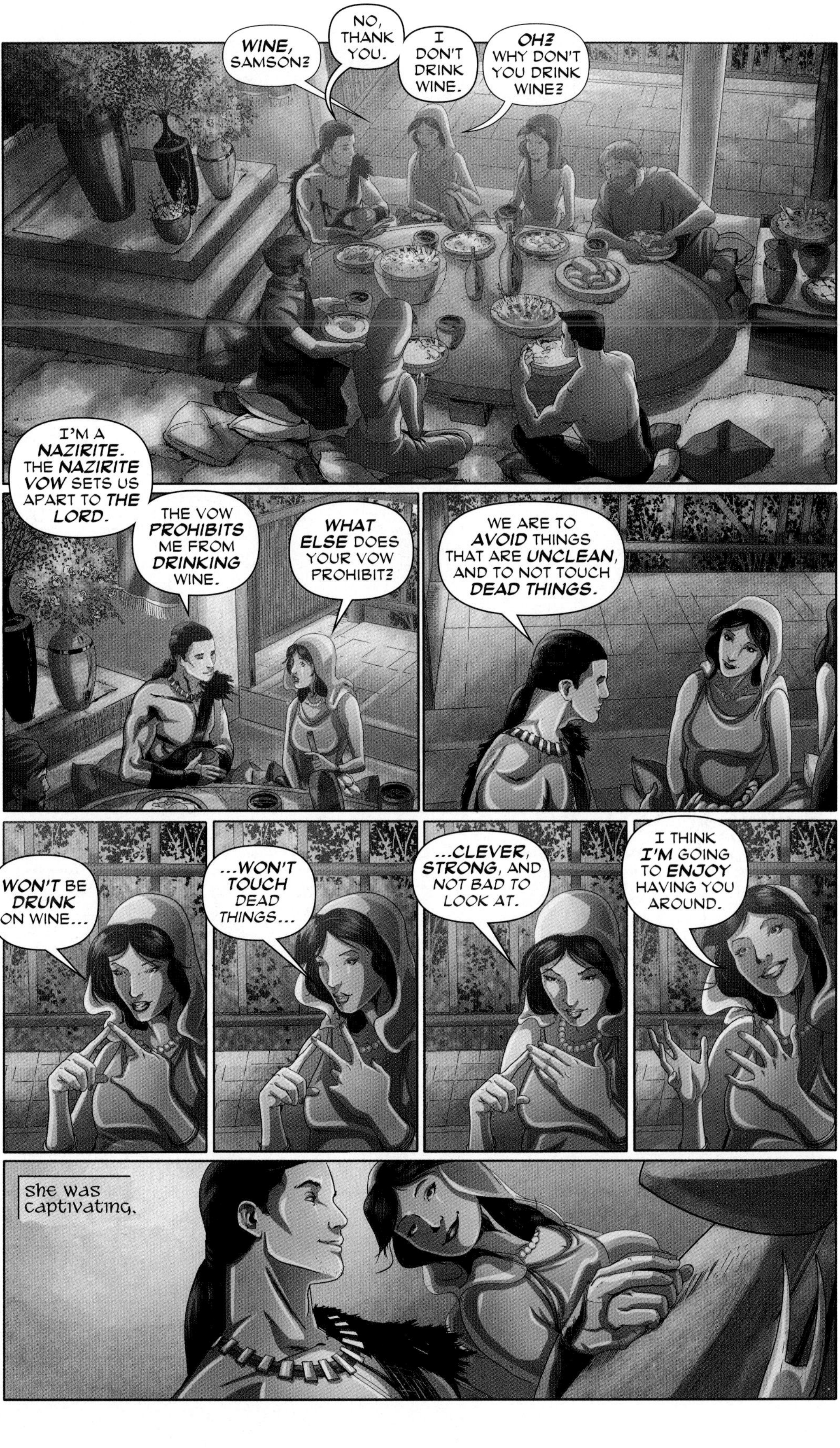
WINE, SAMSON?
NO, THANK YOU.
I DON'T DRINK WINE.
OH? WHY DON'T YOU DRINK WINE?
I'M A NAZIRITE. THE NAZIRITE VOW SETS US APART TO THE LORD.
THE VOW PROHIBITS ME FROM DRINKING WINE.
WHAT ELSE DOES YOUR VOW PROHIBIT?
WE ARE TO AVOID THINGS THAT ARE UNCLEAN, AND TO NOT TOUCH DEAD THINGS.
WON'T BE DRUNK ON WINE...
...WON'T TOUCH DEAD THINGS...
...CLEVER, STRONG, AND NOT BAD TO LOOK AT.
I THINK I'M GOING TO ENJOY HAVING YOU AROUND.
She was captivating.

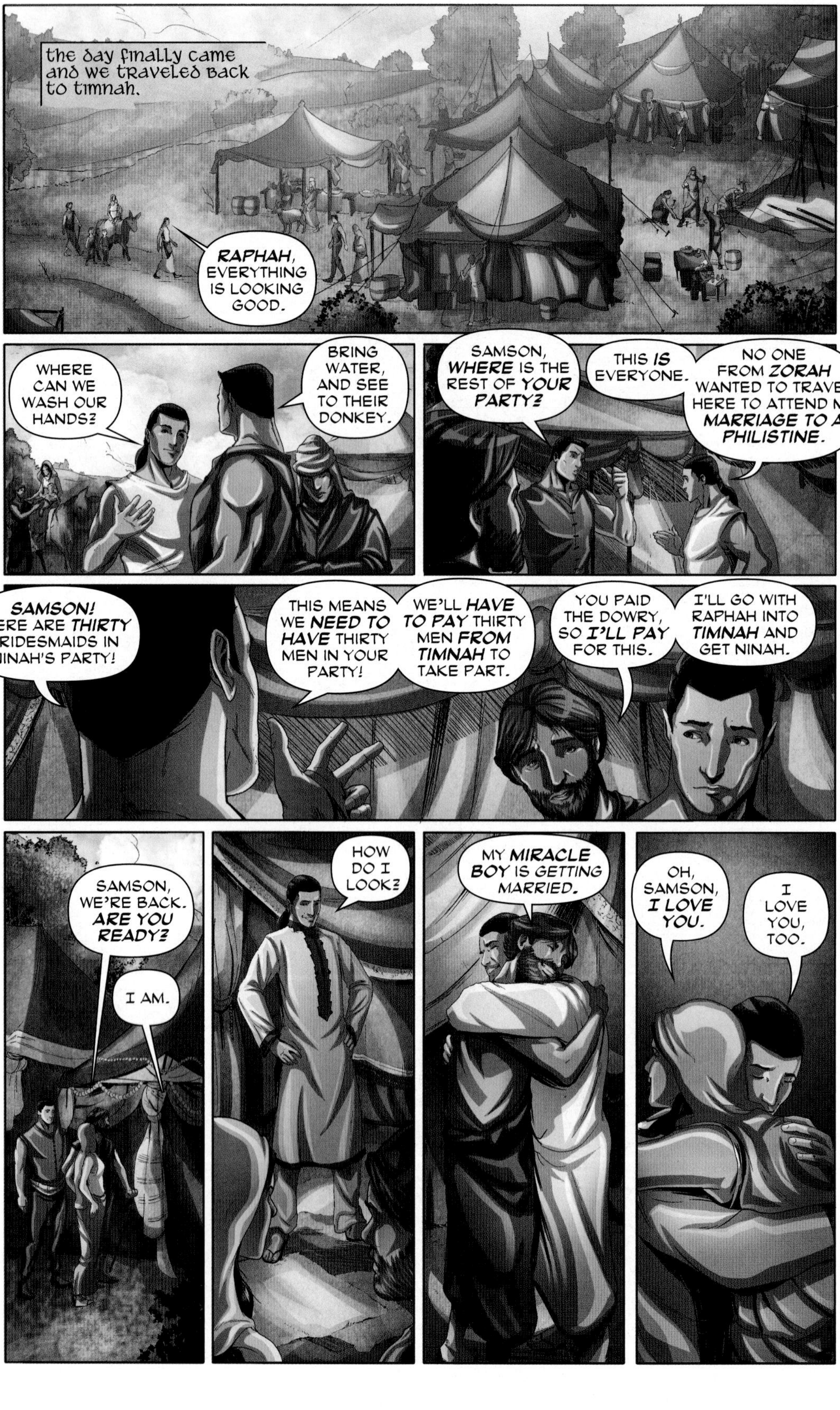
the day finally came and we traveled back to timnah.
RAPHAH, EVERYTHING IS LOOKING GOOD.
WHERE CAN WE WASH OUR HANDS?
BRING WATER, AND SEE TO THEIR DONKEY.
SAMSON, WHERE IS THE REST OF YOUR PARTY?
THIS IS EVERYONE.
NO ONE FROM ZORAH WANTED TO TRAVEL HERE TO ATTEND MY MARRIAGE TO A PHILISTINE.
SAMSON! THERE ARE THIRTY BRIDESMAIDS IN NINAH'S PARTY!
THIS MEANS WE NEED TO HAVE THIRTY MEN IN YOUR PARTY!
WE'LL HAVE TO PAY THIRTY MEN FROM TIMNAH TO TAKE PART.
YOU PAID THE DOWRY, SO I'LL PAY FOR THIS.
I'LL GO WITH RAPHAH INTO TIMNAH AND GET NINAH.
SAMSON, WE'RE BACK. ARE YOU READY?
I AM.
HOW DO I LOOK?
MY MIRACLE BOY IS GETTING MARRIED.
OH, SAMSON, I LOVE YOU.
I LOVE YOU, TOO.

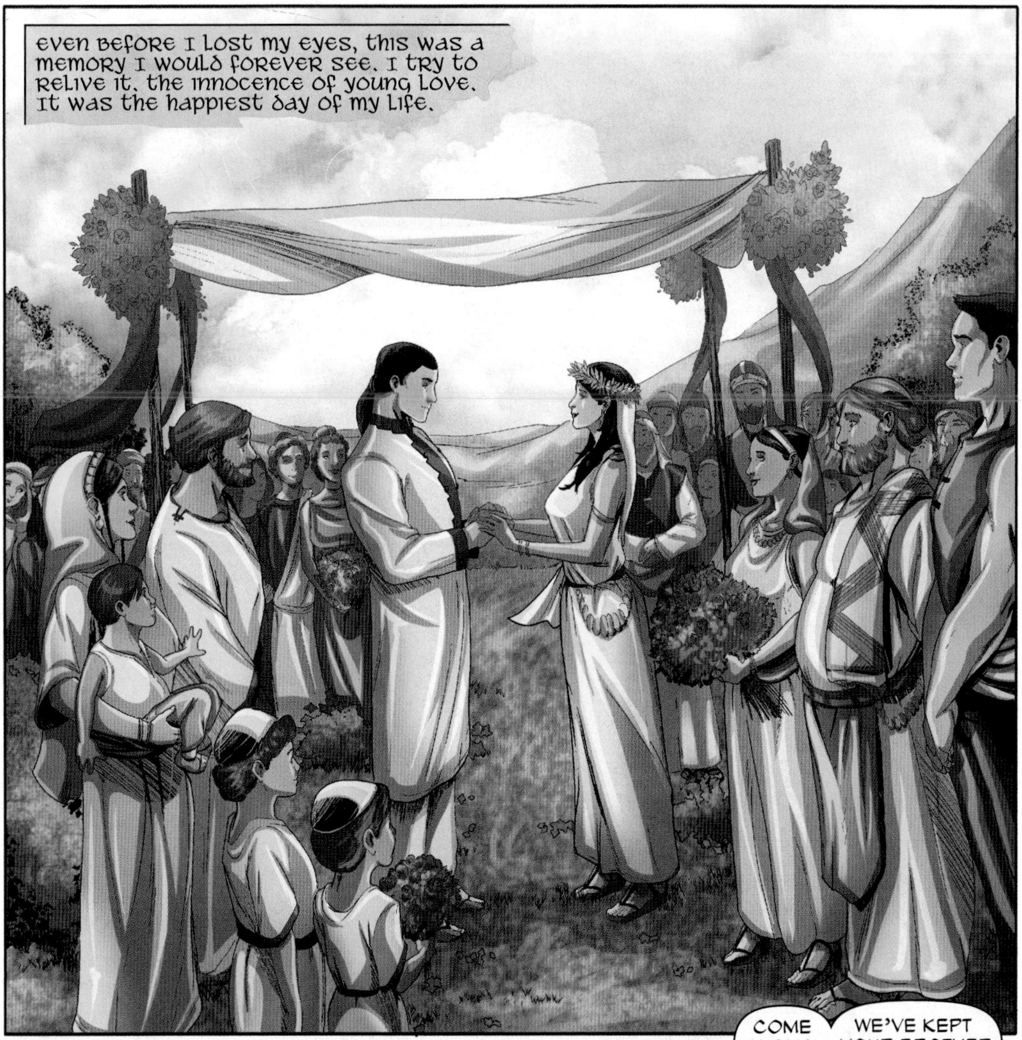
Even before I lost my eyes, this was a memory I would forever see. I try to relive it, the innocence of young love. It was the happiest day of my life.

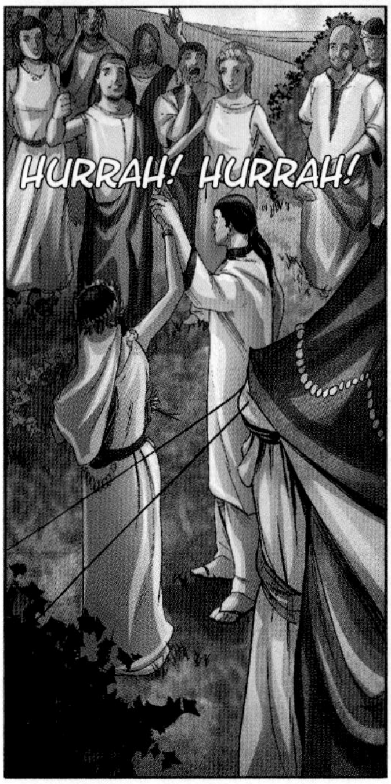
HURRAH! HURRAH!

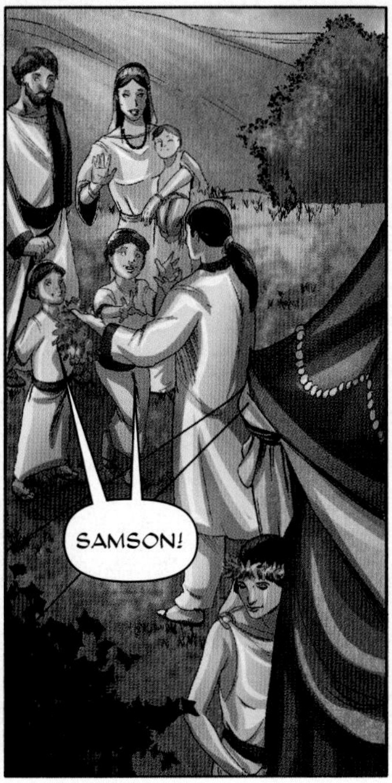
SAMSON!

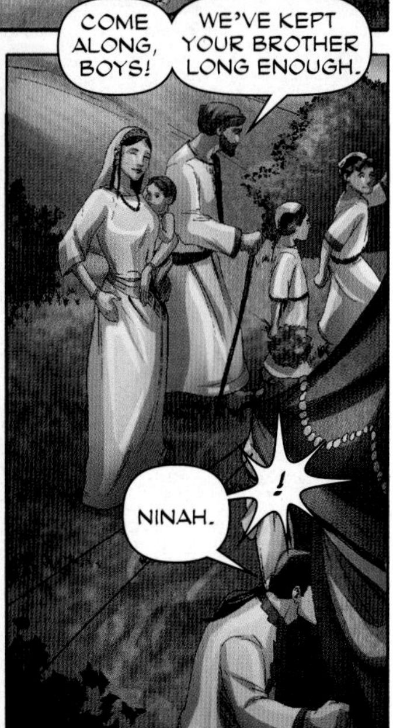
COME ALONG, BOYS!
WE'VE KEPT YOUR BROTHER LONG ENOUGH.
!
NINAH.

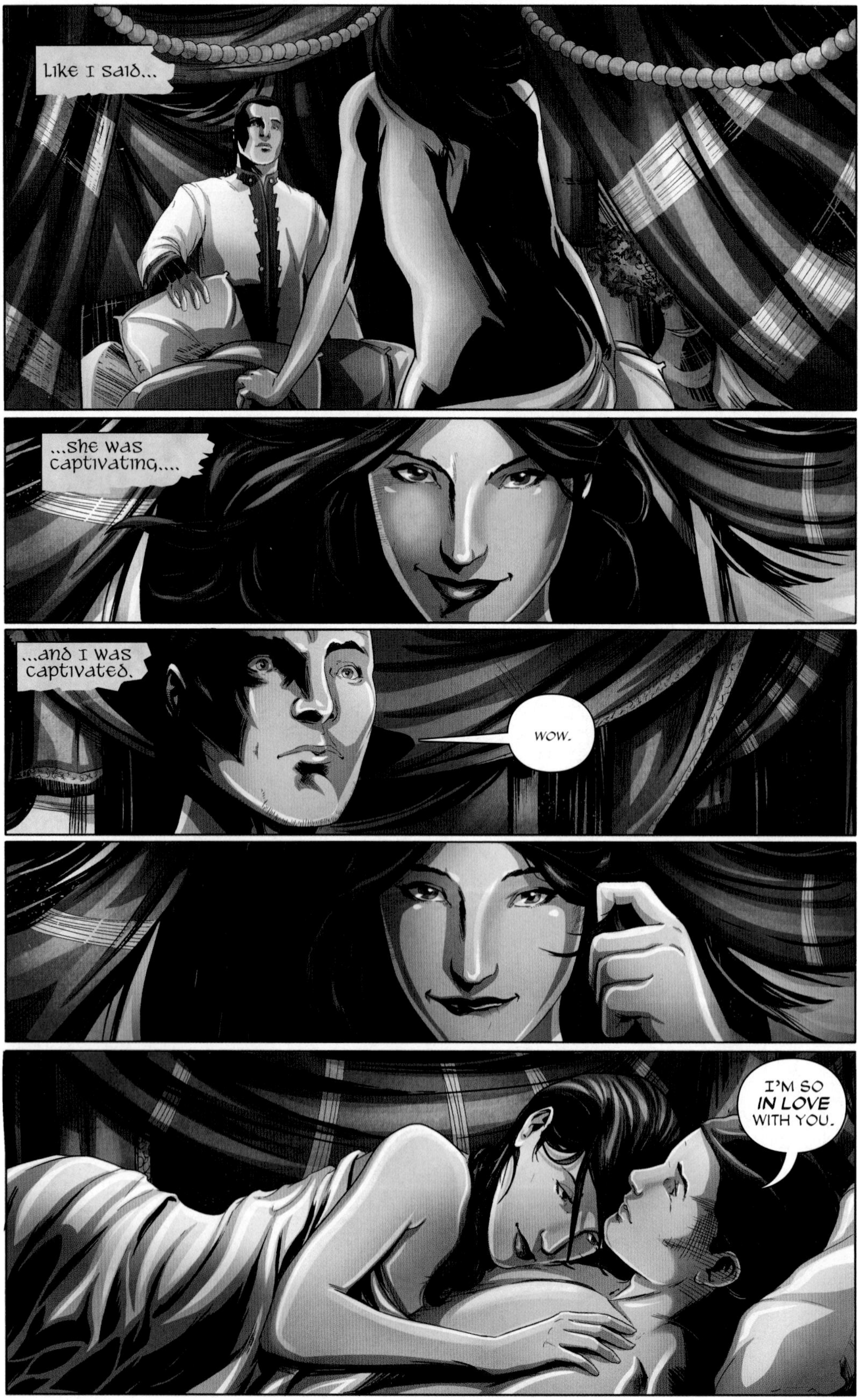
Like I said...
...she was captivating....
...and I was captivated.
WOW.
I'M SO IN LOVE WITH YOU.

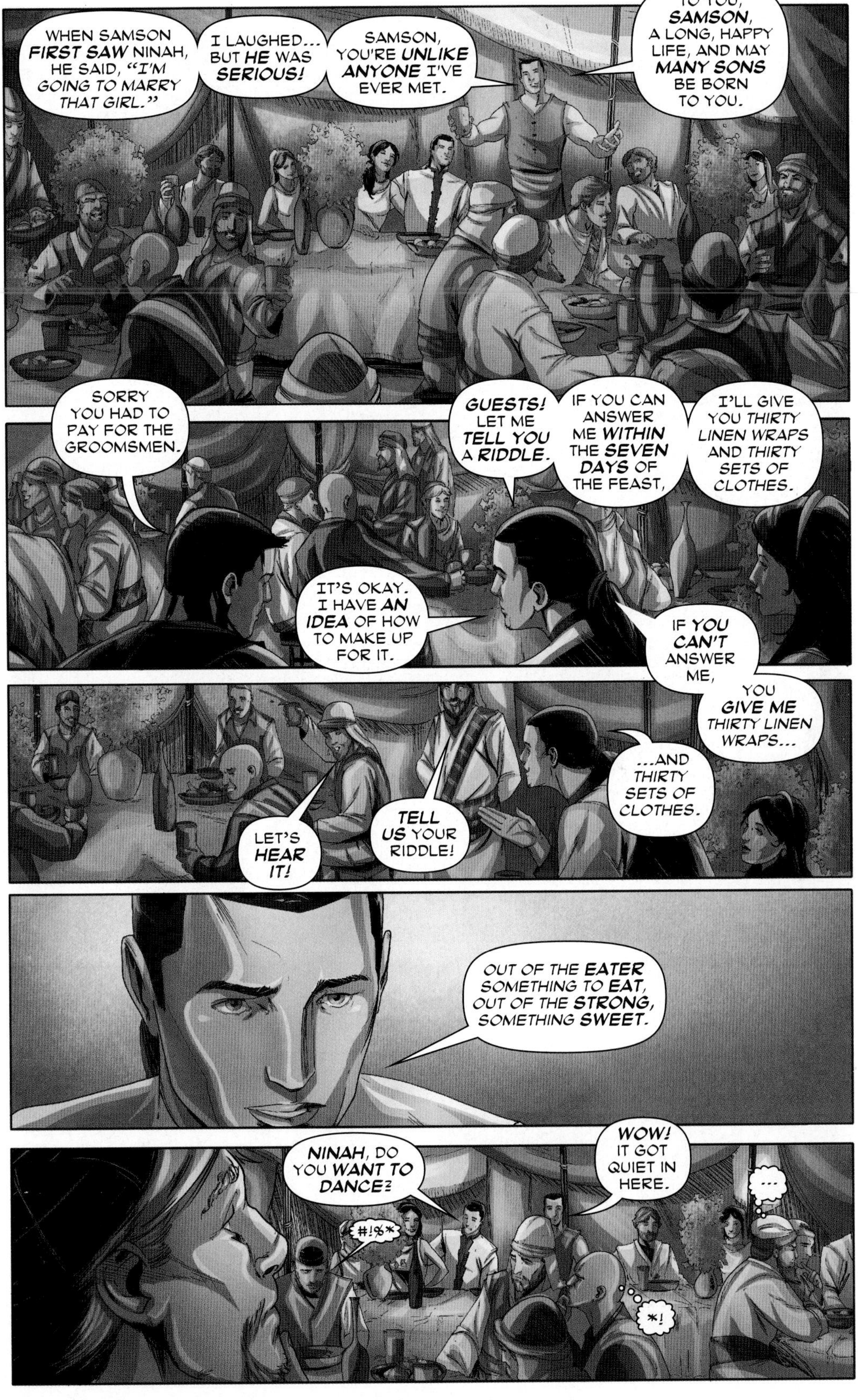
WHEN SAMSON FIRST SAW NINAH, HE SAID, "I'M GOING TO MARRY THAT GIRL."
I LAUGHED... BUT HE WAS SERIOUS!
SAMSON, YOU'RE UNLIKE ANYONE I'VE EVER MET.
TO YOU, SAMSON, A LONG, HAPPY LIFE, AND MAY MANY SONS BE BORN TO YOU.
SORRY YOU HAD TO PAY FOR THE GROOMSMEN.
IT'S OKAY. I HAVE AN IDEA OF HOW TO MAKE UP FOR IT.
GUESTS! LET ME TELL YOU A RIDDLE.
IF YOU CAN ANSWER ME WITHIN THE SEVEN DAYS OF THE FEAST,
I'LL GIVE YOU THIRTY LINEN WRAPS AND THIRTY SETS OF CLOTHES.
IF YOU CAN'T ANSWER ME,
YOU GIVE ME THIRTY LINEN WRAPS...
...AND THIRTY SETS OF CLOTHES.
LET'S HEAR IT!
TELL US YOUR RIDDLE!
OUT OF THE EATER SOMETHING TO EAT, OUT OF THE STRONG, SOMETHING SWEET.
NINAH, DO YOU WANT TO DANCE?
#!%*
WOW! IT GOT QUIET IN HERE.
...
*!

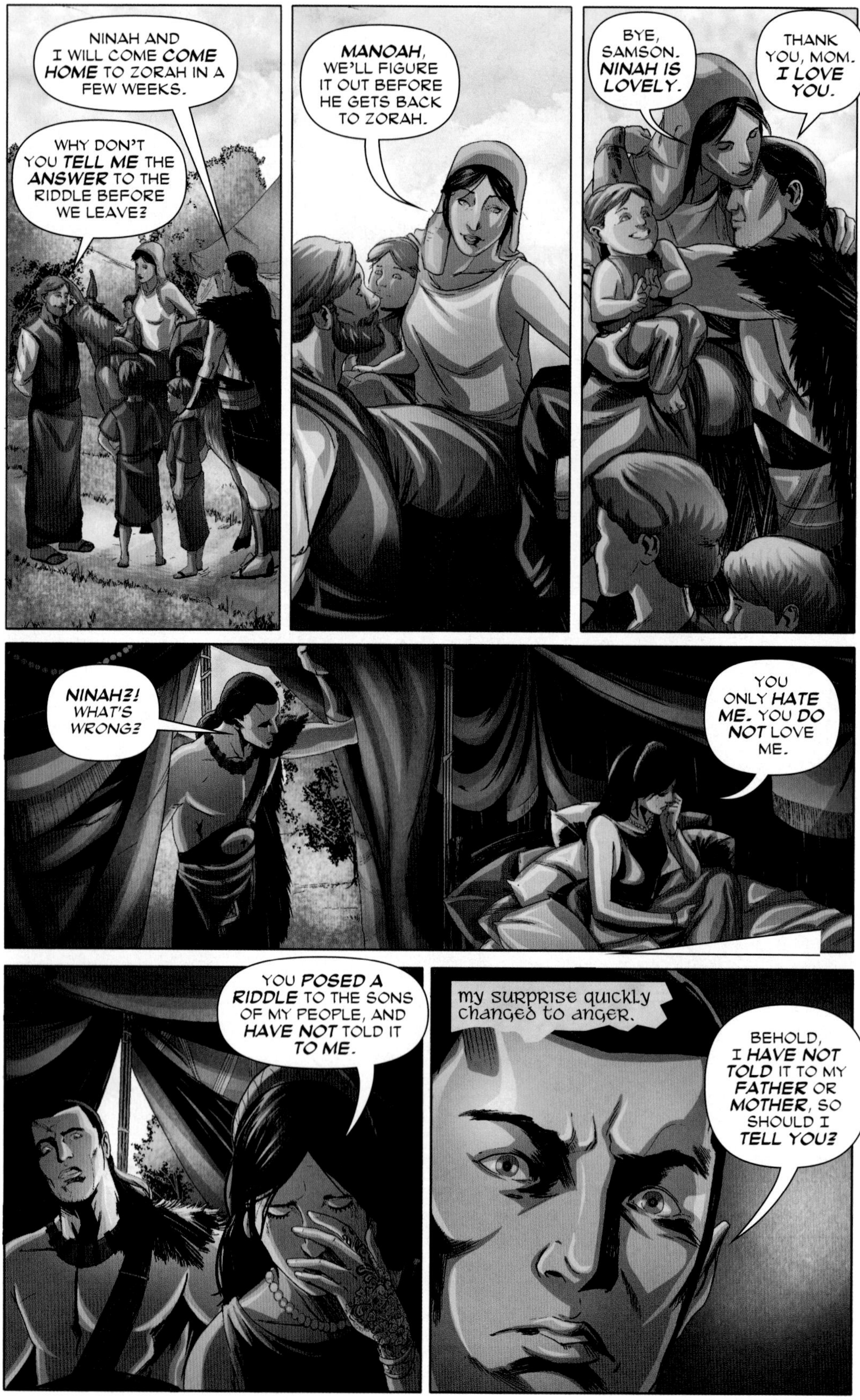
NINAH AND I WILL COME COME HOME TO ZORAH IN A FEW WEEKS.
WHY DON'T YOU TELL ME THE ANSWER TO THE RIDDLE BEFORE WE LEAVE?
MANOAH, WE'LL FIGURE IT OUT BEFORE HE GETS BACK TO ZORAH.
BYE, SAMSON. NINAH IS LOVELY.
THANK YOU, MOM. I LOVE YOU.
NINAH?! WHAT'S WRONG?
YOU ONLY HATE ME. YOU DO NOT LOVE ME.
YOU POSED A RIDDLE TO THE SONS OF MY PEOPLE, AND HAVE NOT TOLD IT TO ME.
my surprise quickly changed to anger.
BEHOLD, I HAVE NOT TOLD IT TO MY FATHER OR MOTHER, SO SHOULD I TELL YOU?

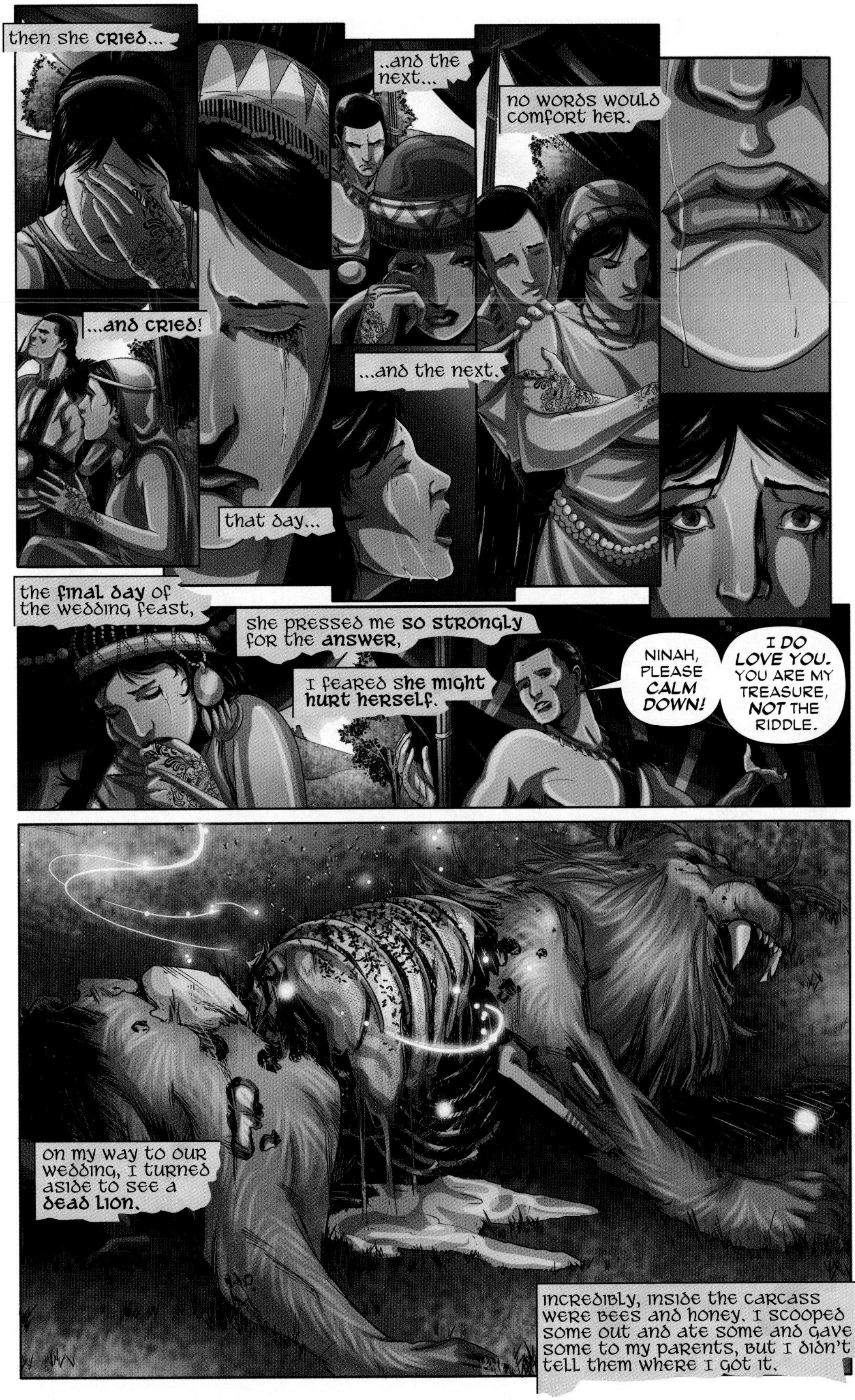
then she cried...
...and cried!
that day...
..and the next...
...and the next.
no words would comfort her.
the final day of the wedding feast,
she pressed me so strongly for the answer,
I feared she might hurt herself.
NINAH, PLEASE CALM DOWN!
I DO LOVE YOU. YOU ARE MY TREASURE, NOT THE RIDDLE.
on my way to our wedding, I turned aside to see a dead lion.
incredibly, inside the carcass were bees and honey. I scooped some out and ate some and gave some to my parents, but I didn't tell them where I got it.

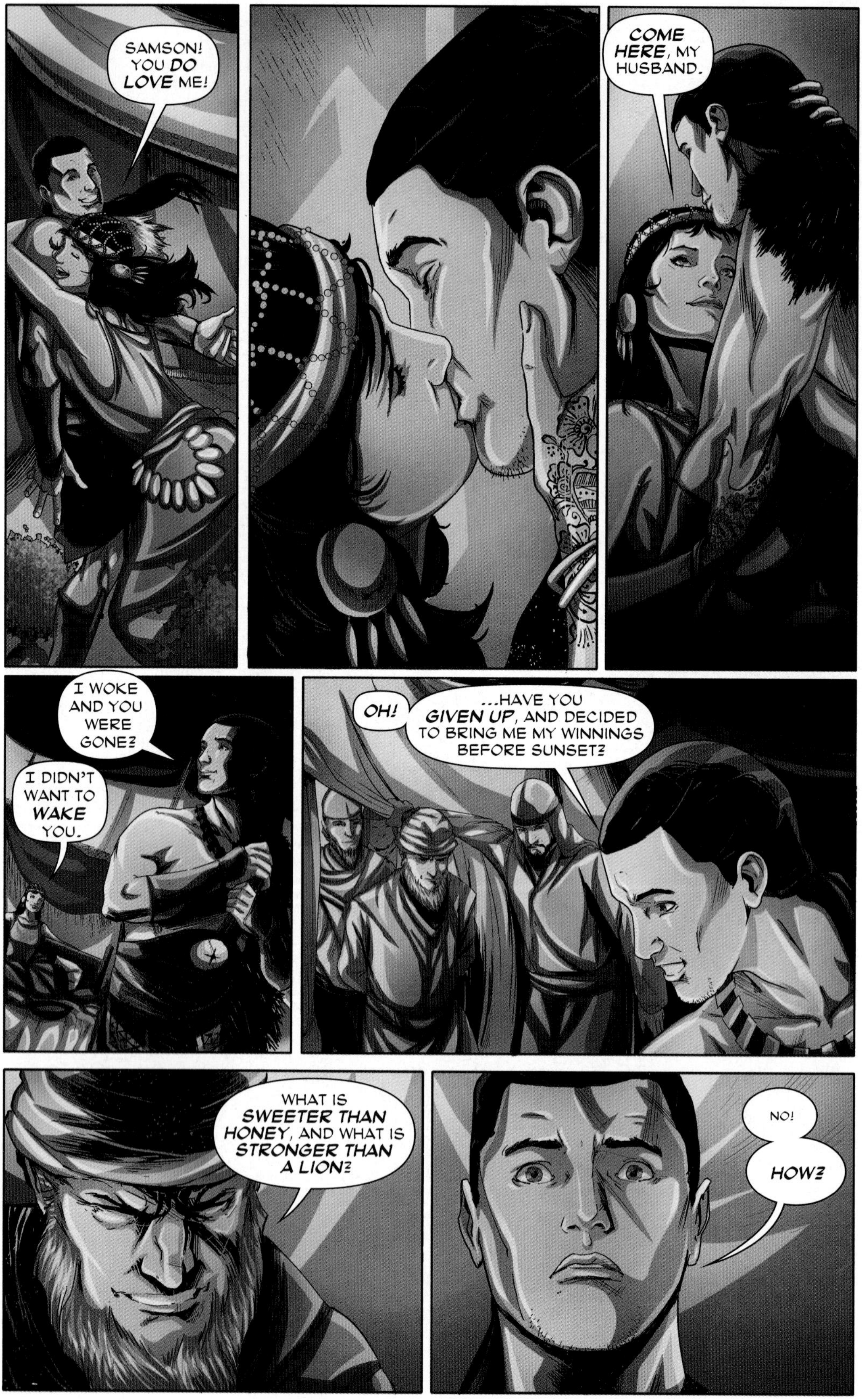
SAMSON! YOU DO LOVE ME!
COME HERE, MY HUSBAND.
I WOKE AND YOU WERE GONE?
I DIDN'T WANT TO WAKE YOU.
OH!
...HAVE YOU GIVEN UP, AND DECIDED TO BRING ME MY WINNINGS BEFORE SUNSET?
WHAT IS SWEETER THAN HONEY, AND WHAT IS STRONGER THAN A LION?
NO!
HOW?

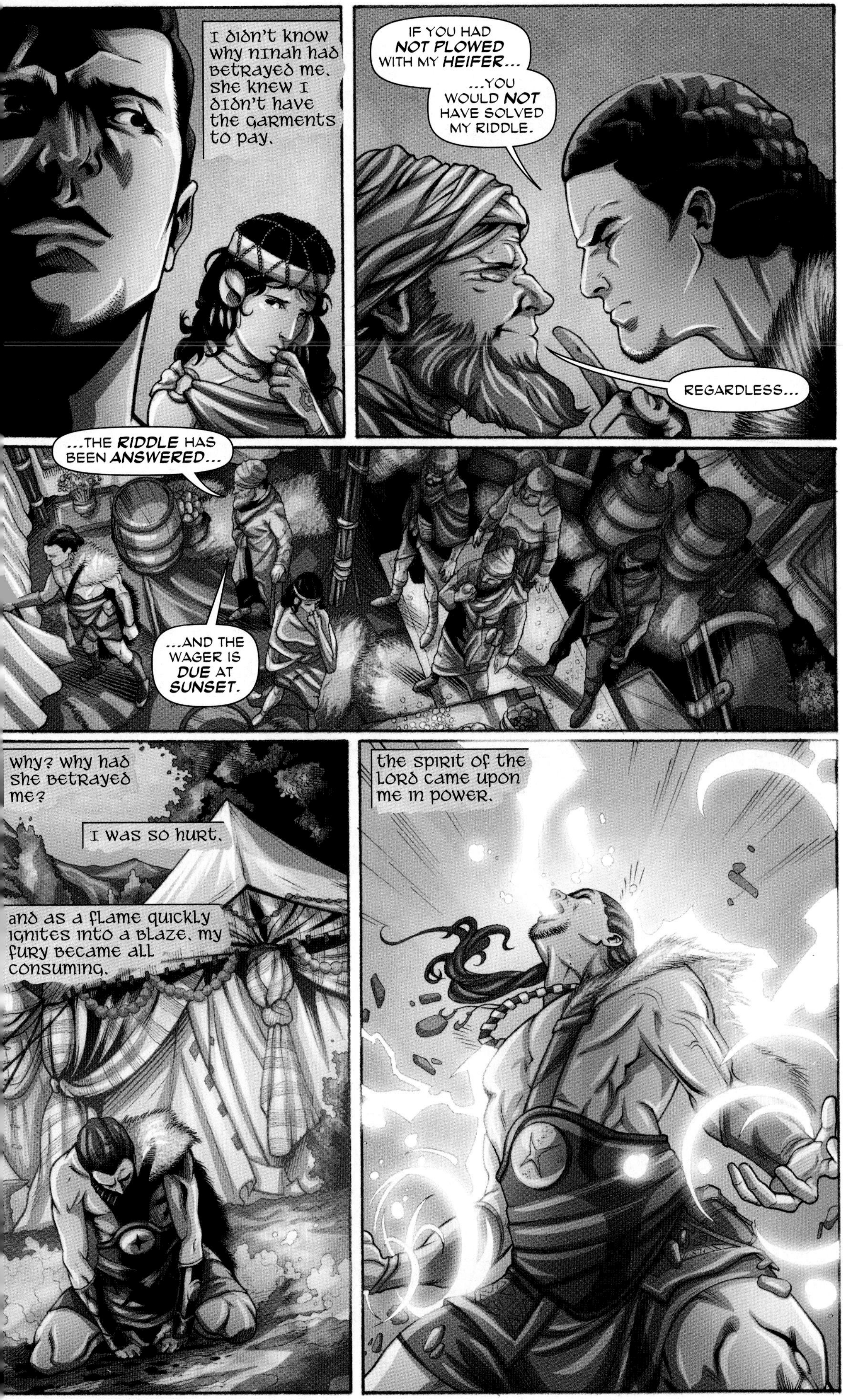
I didn't know why Ninah had betrayed me. She knew I didn't have the garments to pay.
IF YOU HAD NOT PLOWED WITH MY HEIFER...
...YOU WOULD NOT HAVE SOLVED MY RIDDLE.
REGARDLESS...
...THE RIDDLE HAS BEEN ANSWERED...
...AND THE WAGER IS DUE AT SUNSET.
Why? Why had she betrayed me?
I was so hurt.
And as a flame quickly ignites into a blaze, my fury became all consuming.
The Spirit of the Lord came upon me in power.

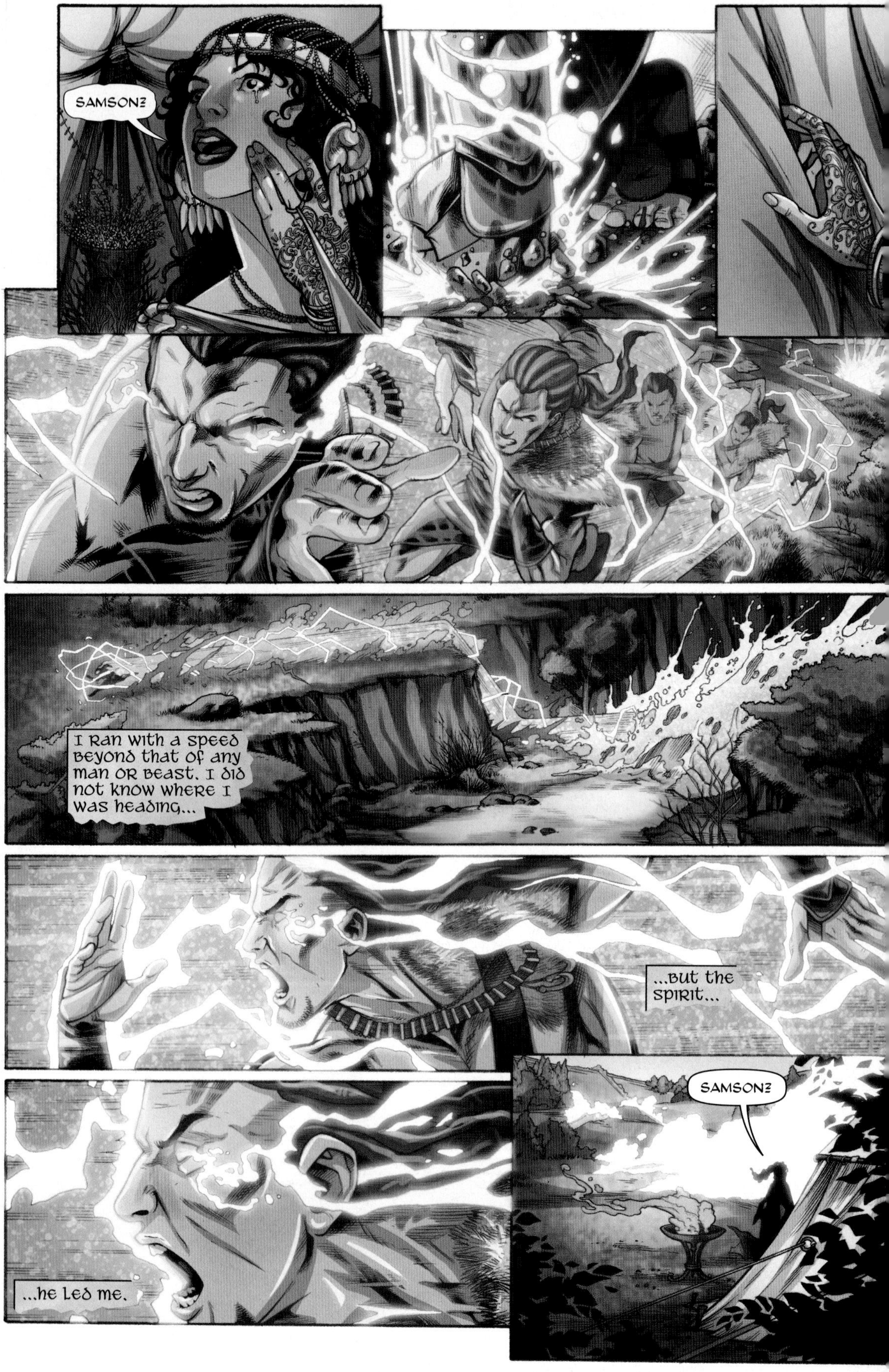
SAMSON?
I Ran with a speed beyond that of any man or beast. I did not know where I was heading...
...but the spirit...
...he led me.
SAMSON?

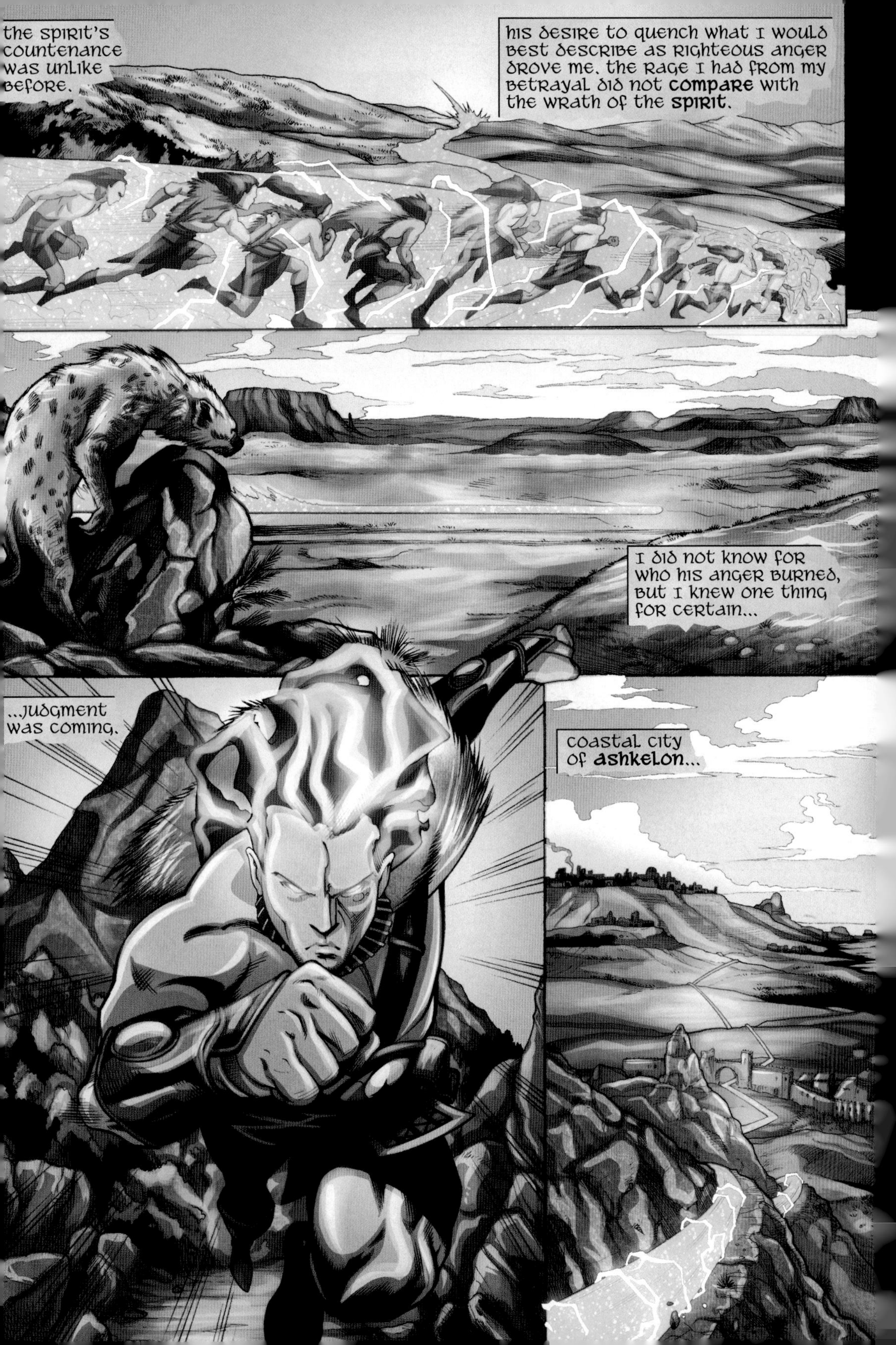
the spirit's countenance was unlike before.
his desire to quench what I would best describe as righteous anger drove me. the rage I had from my betrayal did not **compare** with the wrath of the **spirit**.
I did not know for who his anger burned, but I knew one thing for certain...
...judgment was coming.
coastal city of **ashkelon**...

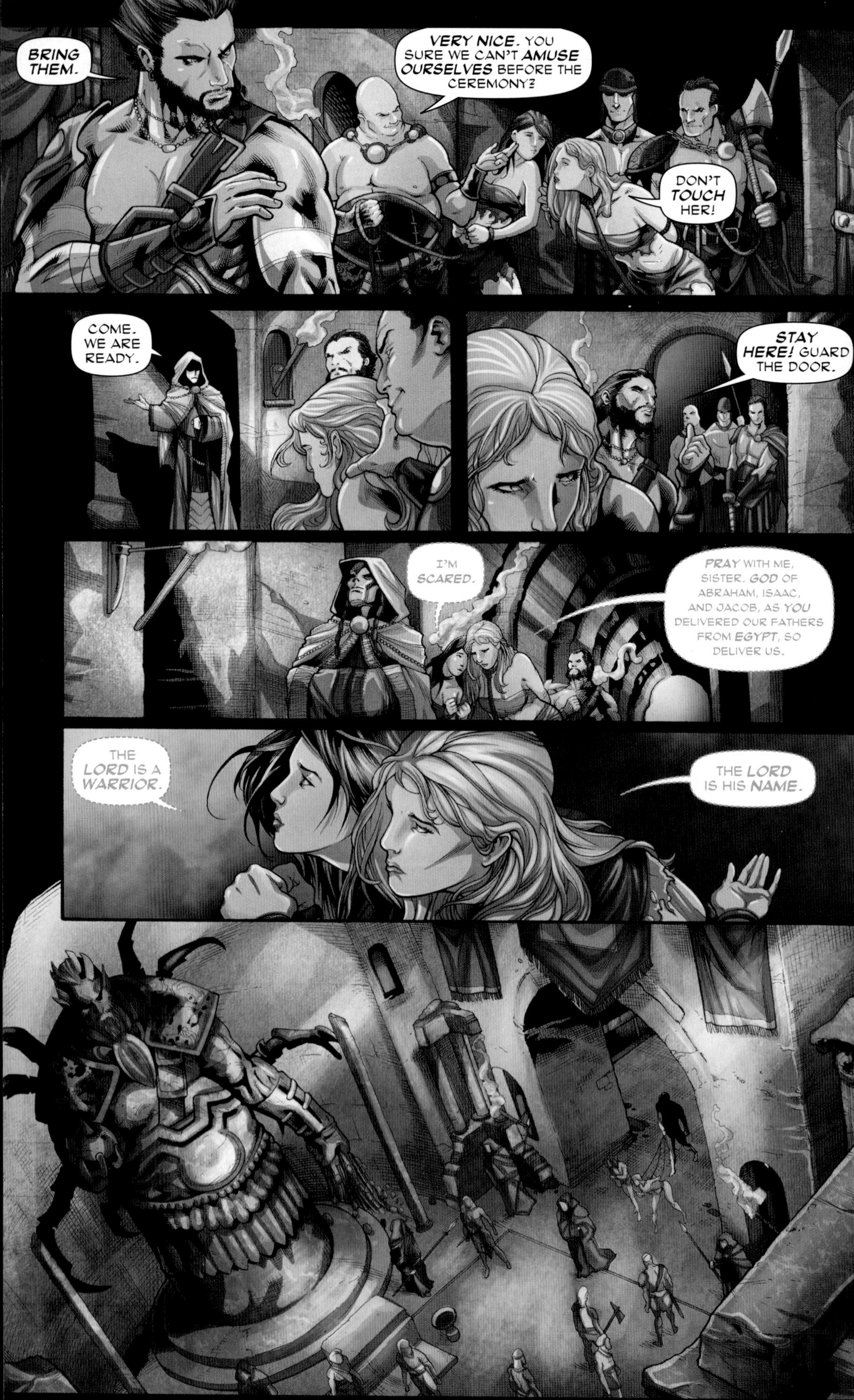
BRING THEM.
VERY NICE. YOU SURE WE CAN'T AMUSE OURSELVES BEFORE THE CEREMONY?
DON'T TOUCH HER!
COME. WE ARE READY.
STAY HERE! GUARD THE DOOR.
I'M SCARED.
PRAY WITH ME, SISTER. GOD OF ABRAHAM, ISAAC, AND JACOB, AS YOU DELIVERED OUR FATHERS FROM EGYPT, SO DELIVER US.
THE LORD IS A WARRIOR.
THE LORD IS HIS NAME.

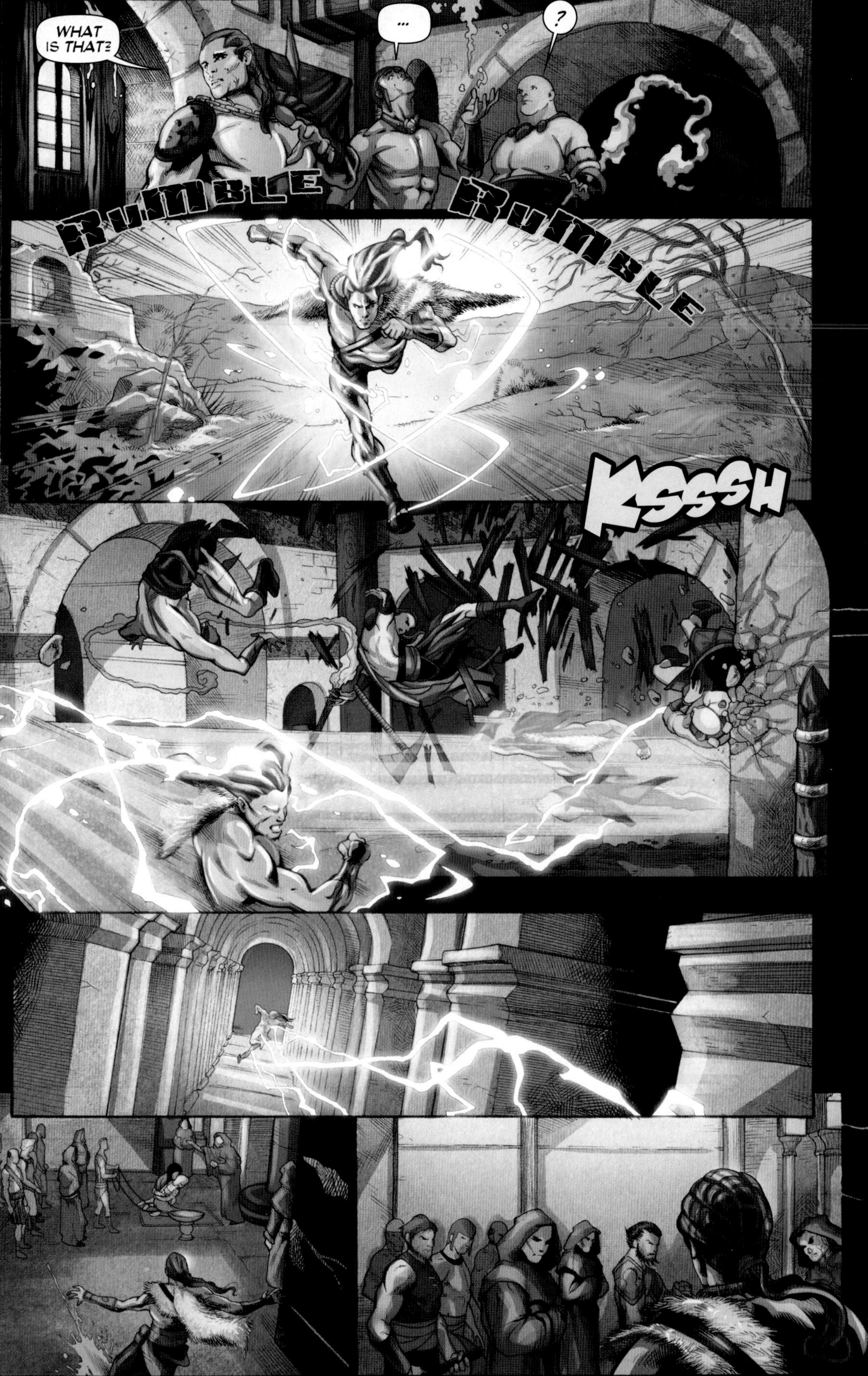
WHAT IS THAT?
...
?
RUMBLE RUMBLE
KSSSH

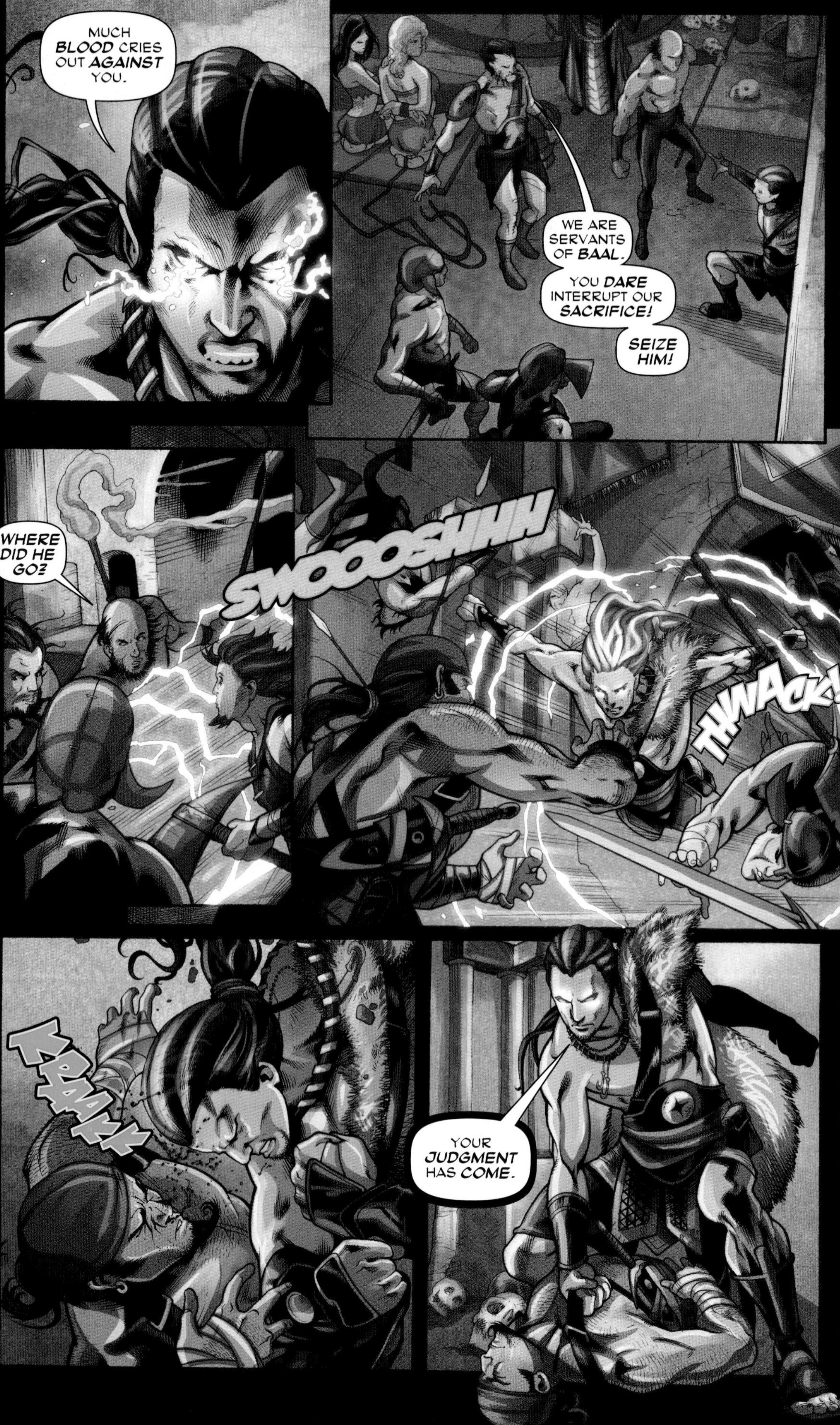
MUCH BLOOD CRIES OUT AGAINST YOU.
WE ARE SERVANTS OF BAAL.
YOU DARE INTERRUPT OUR SACRIFICE!
SEIZE HIM!
WHERE DID HE GO?
SWOOOOSHHH
THWACK!
KRAAKK
YOUR JUDGMENT HAS COME.

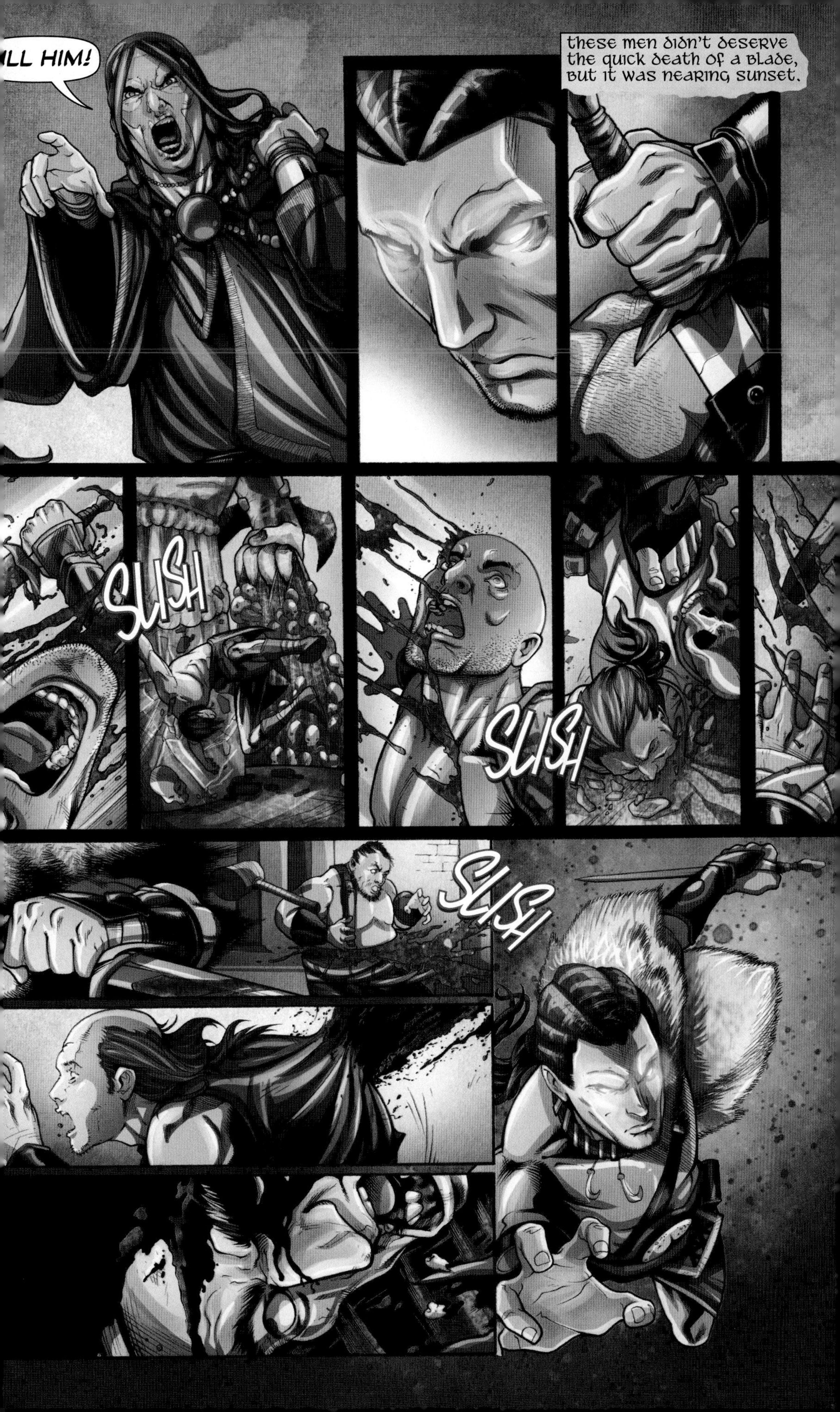

ILL HIM!
these men didn't deserve the quick death of a blade, but it was nearing sunset.
SLISH
SLISH
SLISH

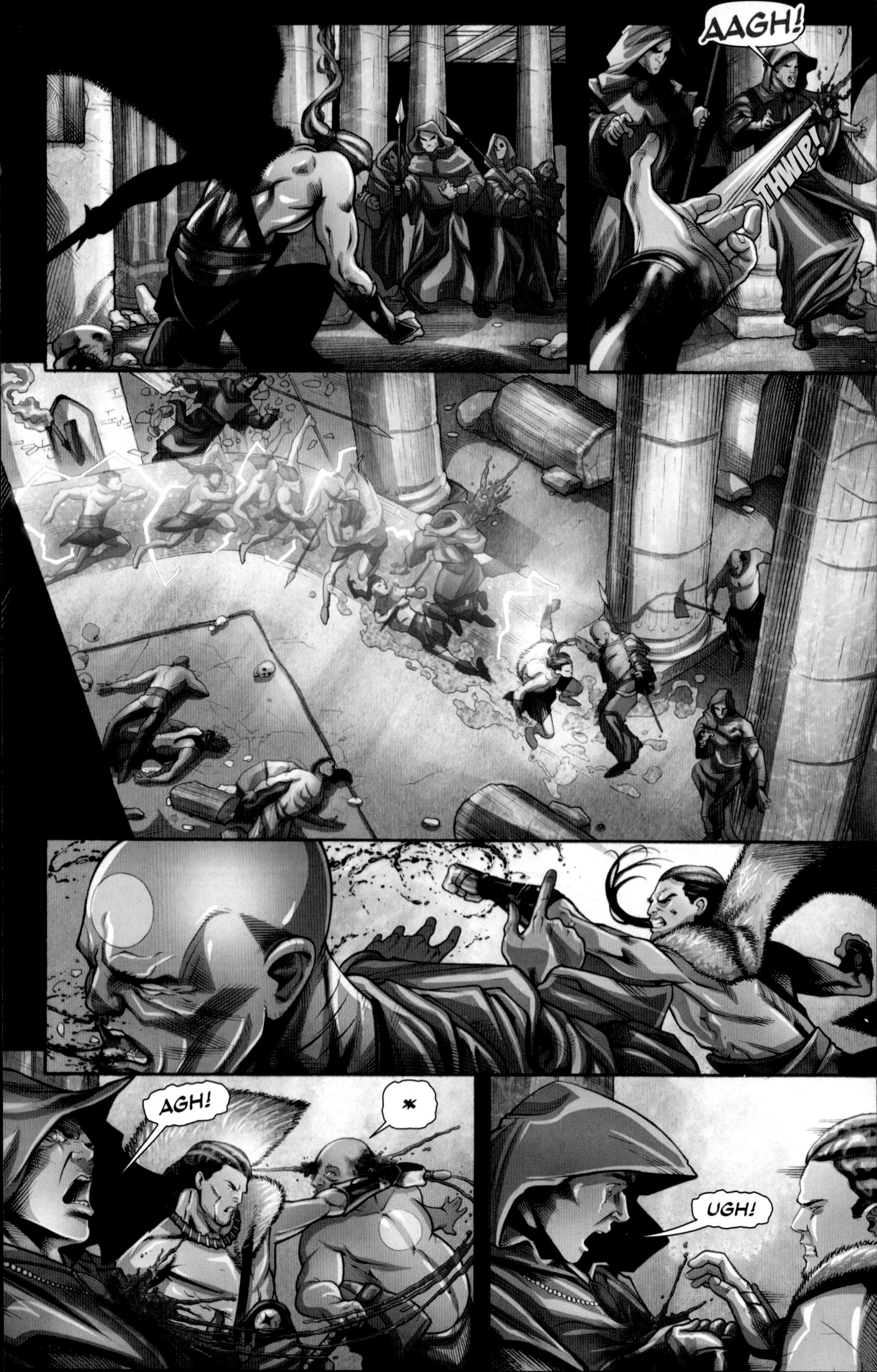
AAGH!
THWIP!
AGH!
*
UGH!

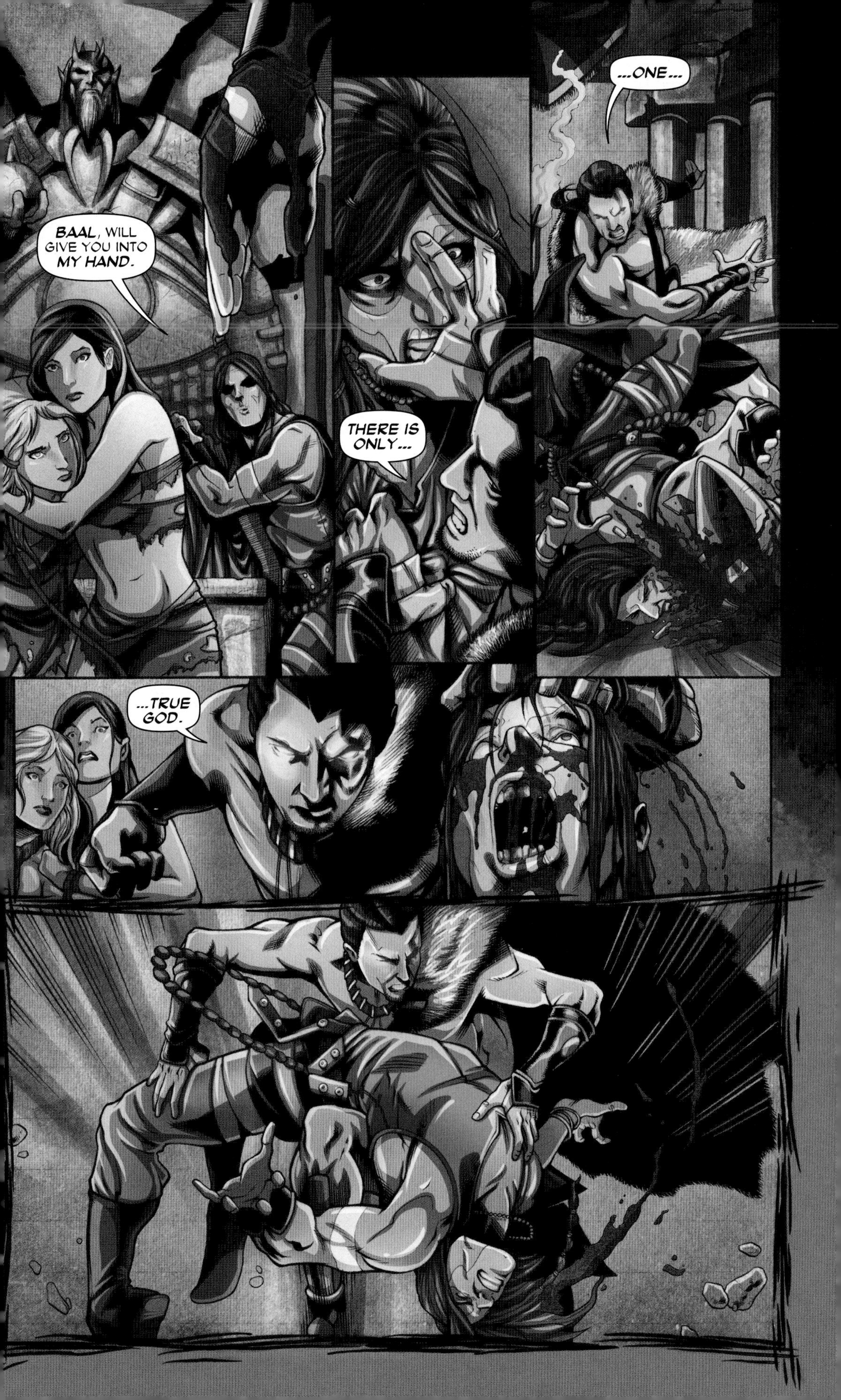
BAAL, WILL GIVE YOU INTO MY HAND.
THERE IS ONLY...
...ONE...
...TRUE GOD.

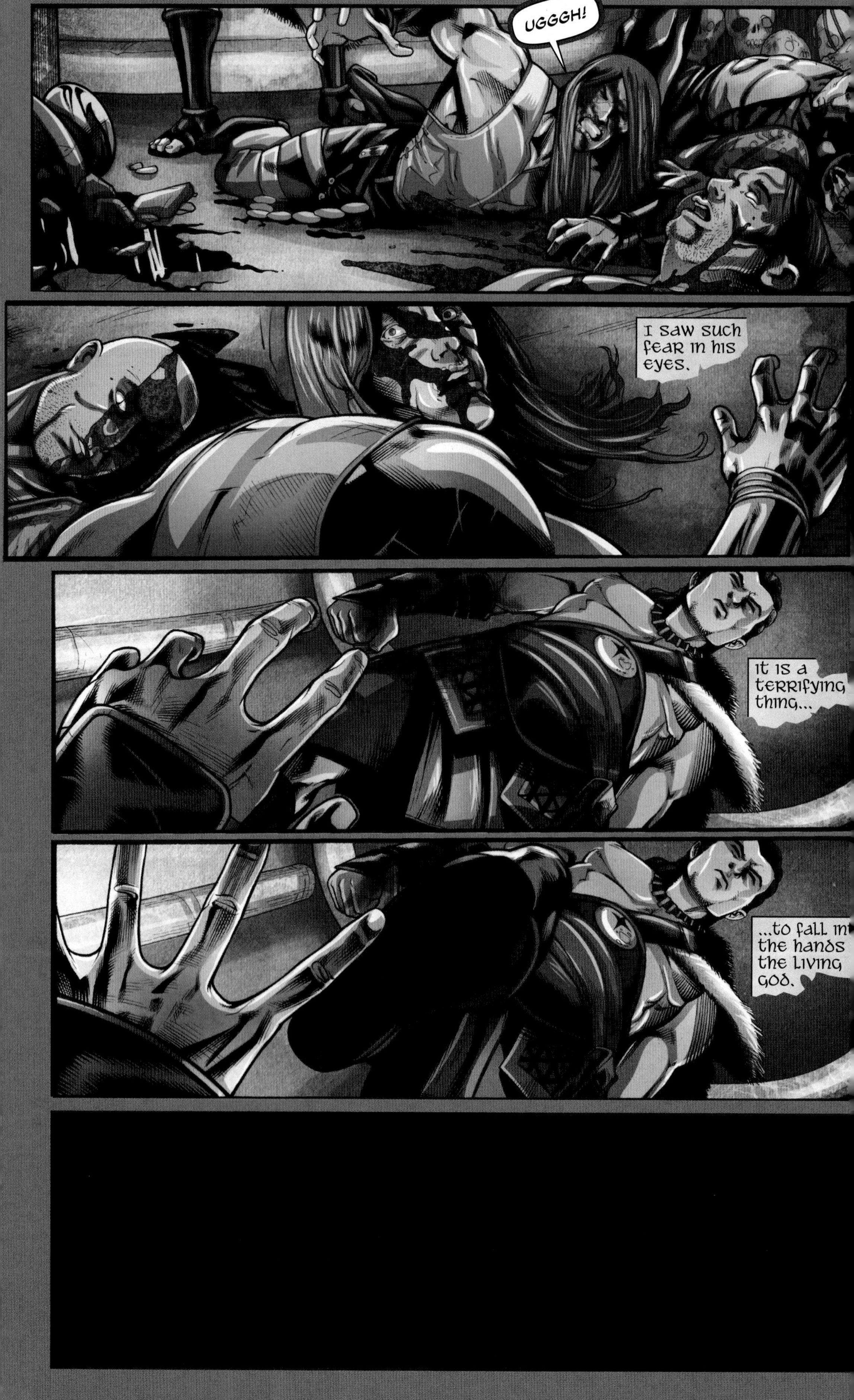
UGGGH!
I saw such fear in his eyes.
It is a terrifying thing...
...to fall in the hands the living god.

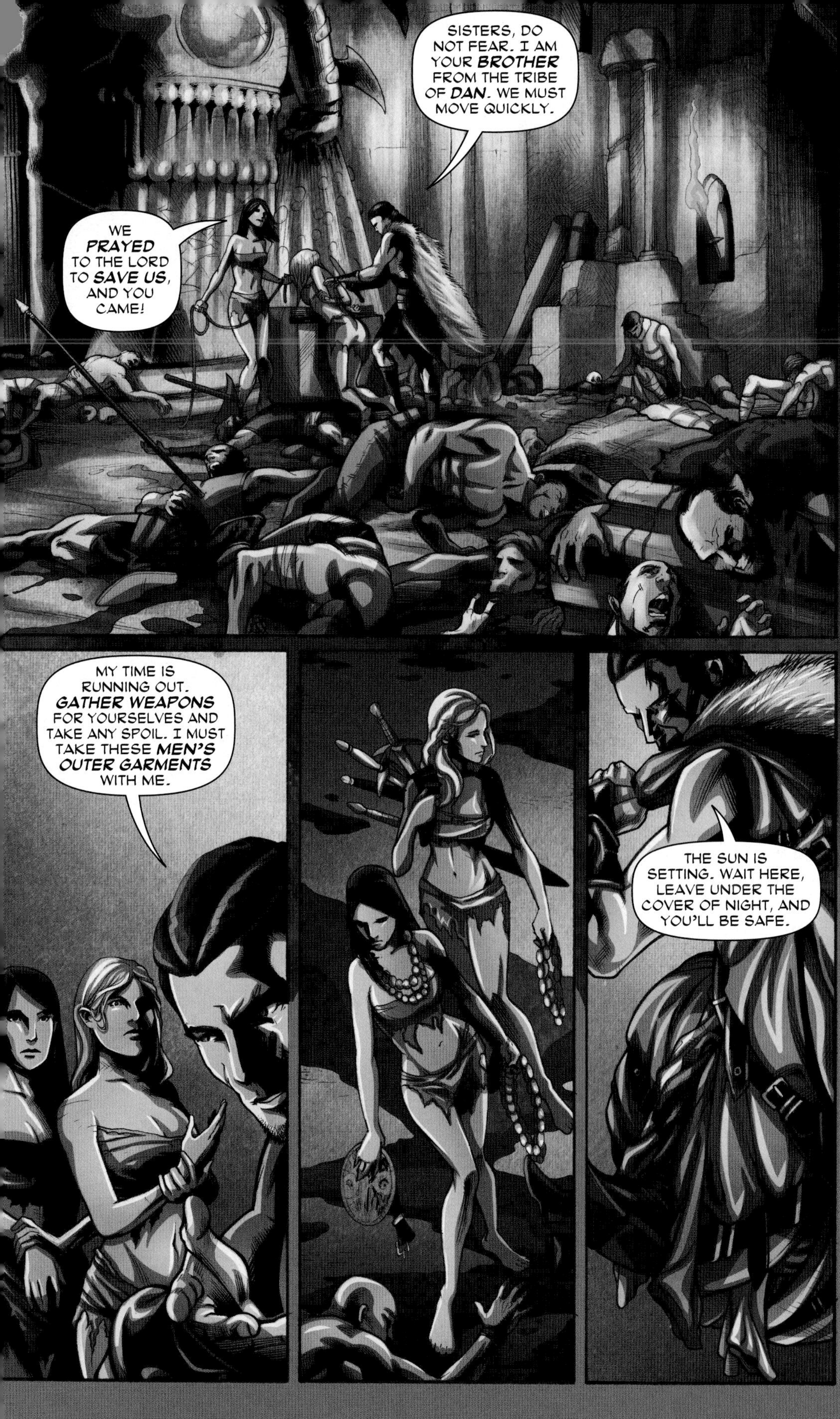
SISTERS, DO NOT FEAR. I AM YOUR BROTHER FROM THE TRIBE OF DAN. WE MUST MOVE QUICKLY.
WE PRAYED TO THE LORD TO SAVE US, AND YOU CAME!
MY TIME IS RUNNING OUT. GATHER WEAPONS FOR YOURSELVES AND TAKE ANY SPOIL. I MUST TAKE THESE MEN'S OUTER GARMENTS WITH ME.
THE SUN IS SETTING. WAIT HERE, LEAVE UNDER THE COVER OF NIGHT, AND YOU'LL BE SAFE.

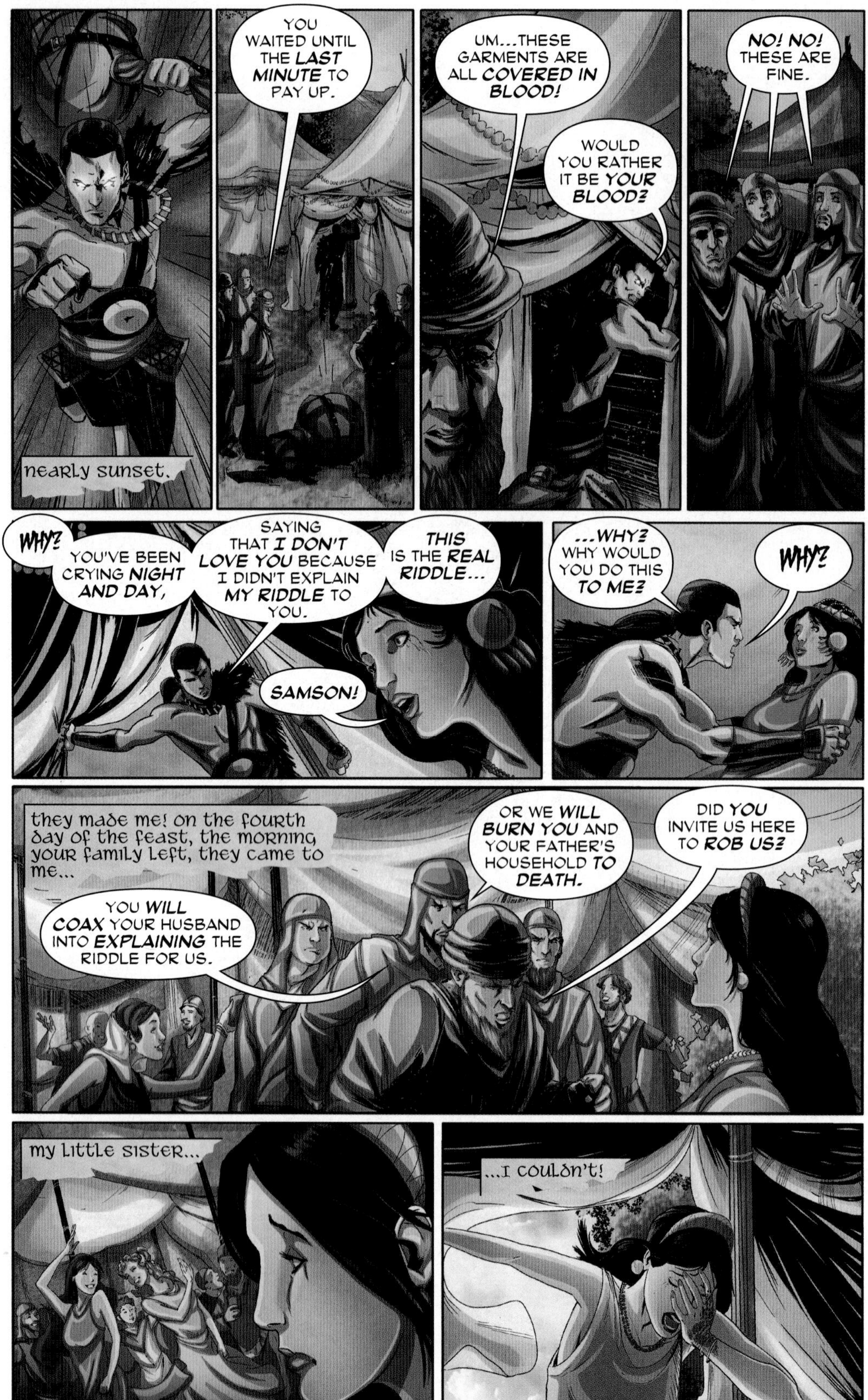
nearly sunset.
YOU WAITED UNTIL THE LAST MINUTE TO PAY UP.
UM... THESE GARMENTS ARE ALL COVERED IN BLOOD!
WOULD YOU RATHER IT BE YOUR BLOOD?
NO! NO! THESE ARE FINE.
WHY?
YOU'VE BEEN CRYING NIGHT AND DAY,
SAYING THAT I DON'T LOVE YOU BECAUSE I DIDN'T EXPLAIN MY RIDDLE TO YOU.
THIS IS THE REAL RIDDLE...
SAMSON!
...WHY? WHY WOULD YOU DO THIS TO ME?
WHY?
they made me! on the fourth day of the feast, the morning your family left, they came to me...
YOU WILL COAX YOUR HUSBAND INTO EXPLAINING THE RIDDLE FOR US.
OR WE WILL BURN YOU AND YOUR FATHER'S HOUSEHOLD TO DEATH.
DID YOU INVITE US HERE TO ROB US?
my little sister...
...I couldn't!

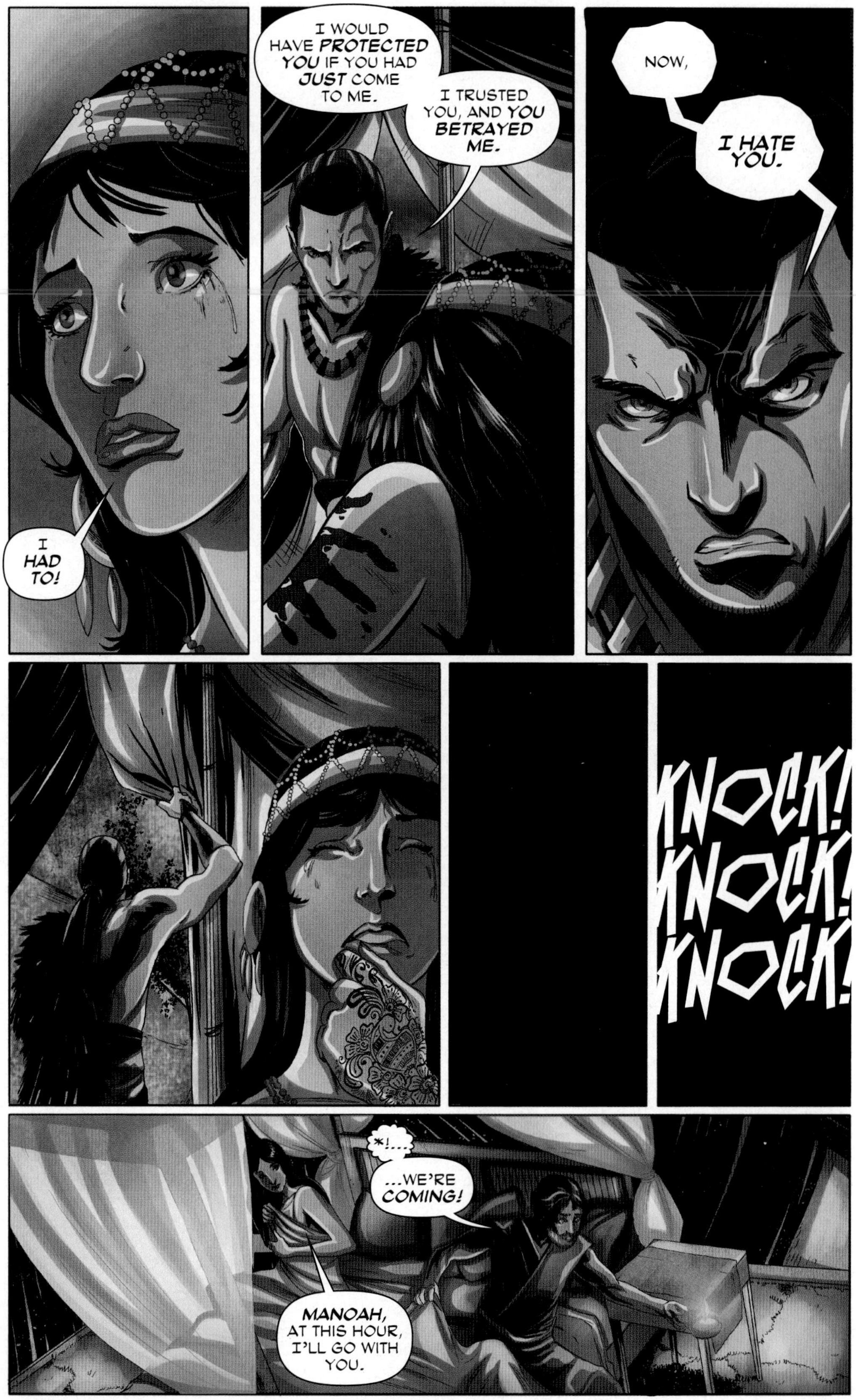
I HAD TO!
I WOULD HAVE PROTECTED YOU IF YOU HAD JUST COME TO ME.
I TRUSTED YOU, AND YOU BETRAYED ME.
NOW,
I HATE YOU.
KNOCK! KNOCK! KNOCK!
*!...
...WE'RE COMING!
MANOAH, AT THIS HOUR, I'LL GO WITH YOU.

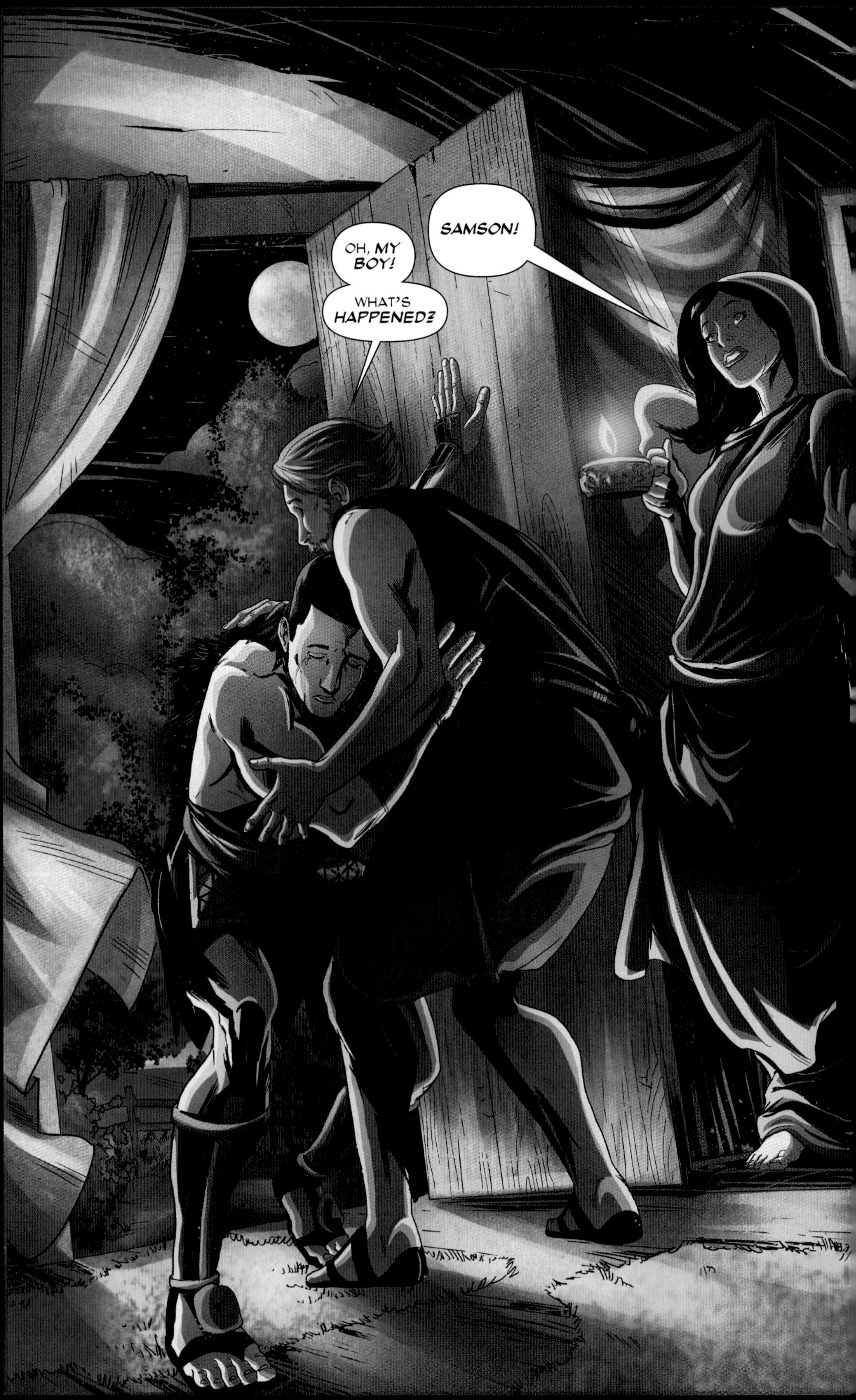
SAMSON!
OH, MY BOY!
WHAT'S HAPPENED?

Letter to the Reader

'Oh, my boy! What's happened?' I love ending this volume with that question. We hope the follow up question is: 'What's going to happen next?'

First and foremost, thank you for taking the time to read **Volume 1, 'Samson the Nazirite'**. We sincerely hope that you enjoyed this story.

So what's next?

'Samson the Nazirite' will be a three volume series based on the book of Judges Chapters 13 – 16. We are striving to stay in line with the biblical account, so if you want to find out what ends up happening you can jump ahead and read it there.

If you've enjoyed this volume and want to read the next volumes, then please join us in making that happen. Of course we need money, but more important is positive word of mouth. Support can also be an encouraging email, a recommendation to friends, a positive review, a 'like', +1, tweet, even a head nod if you pass me on the street. Whatever you like.

Instead of pitching this to a publisher, we're pitching it to the people. This is our pilot. Are there enough people who enjoy this and will get behind it? We think so.

Thank you's:

We've had a great team on this project and excellent people who have contributed in a variety of ways. I'd like to specifically recognize three people, without whom this project wouldn't have happened:

Nadir Balan (Penciller/Inker) – Thank you for not only your beautiful pages, but for all the extra time and effort you put in. Your work speaks for itself. I recommend a second, slower reading of this book, in order to appreciate the detail he poured into these pages.

Tiffany Serrano – My beloved. This flat out doesn't happen without you. Your support throughout this journey is an amazing act(s) of love. I am forever grateful.

Heavenly Father – For showing me that the process has seasons and that they take their time. Teaching me to trust during seasons of waiting. Thank you for using imperfect people, and your loving kindness.

-Luis Serrano *(creator/writer)*

Rooted Chronicles is our publishing arm. We hope to publish many more Bible based titles. There is great beauty in the Scriptures, which is one of the reasons it's the world's best-selling book of all time. There are rich characters and wonderful stories all throughout it. It has inspired for generations, and will continue to inspire for generations to come.

Visit our website: **RootedChronicles.com**

Naturally, we recommend adding it to your favorites! We add a variety of content regularly, and you can find out more about us there.

Samson the Nazirite also has it's own website;
SamsonTN.com

We've included Cover Art and Concept Art in the following pages, ending with our teaser Cover for Volume 2!

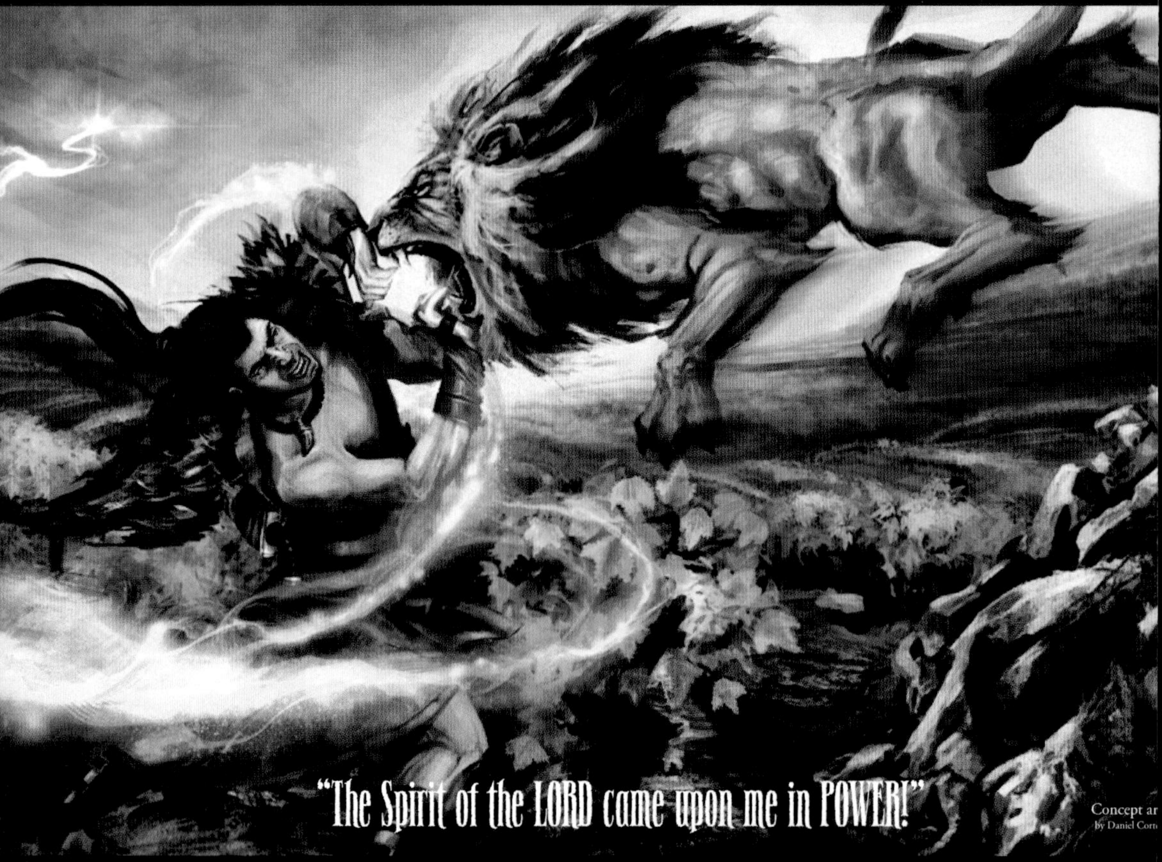
"The Spirit of the LORD came upon me in POWER!"

Concept ar
by Daniel Corto

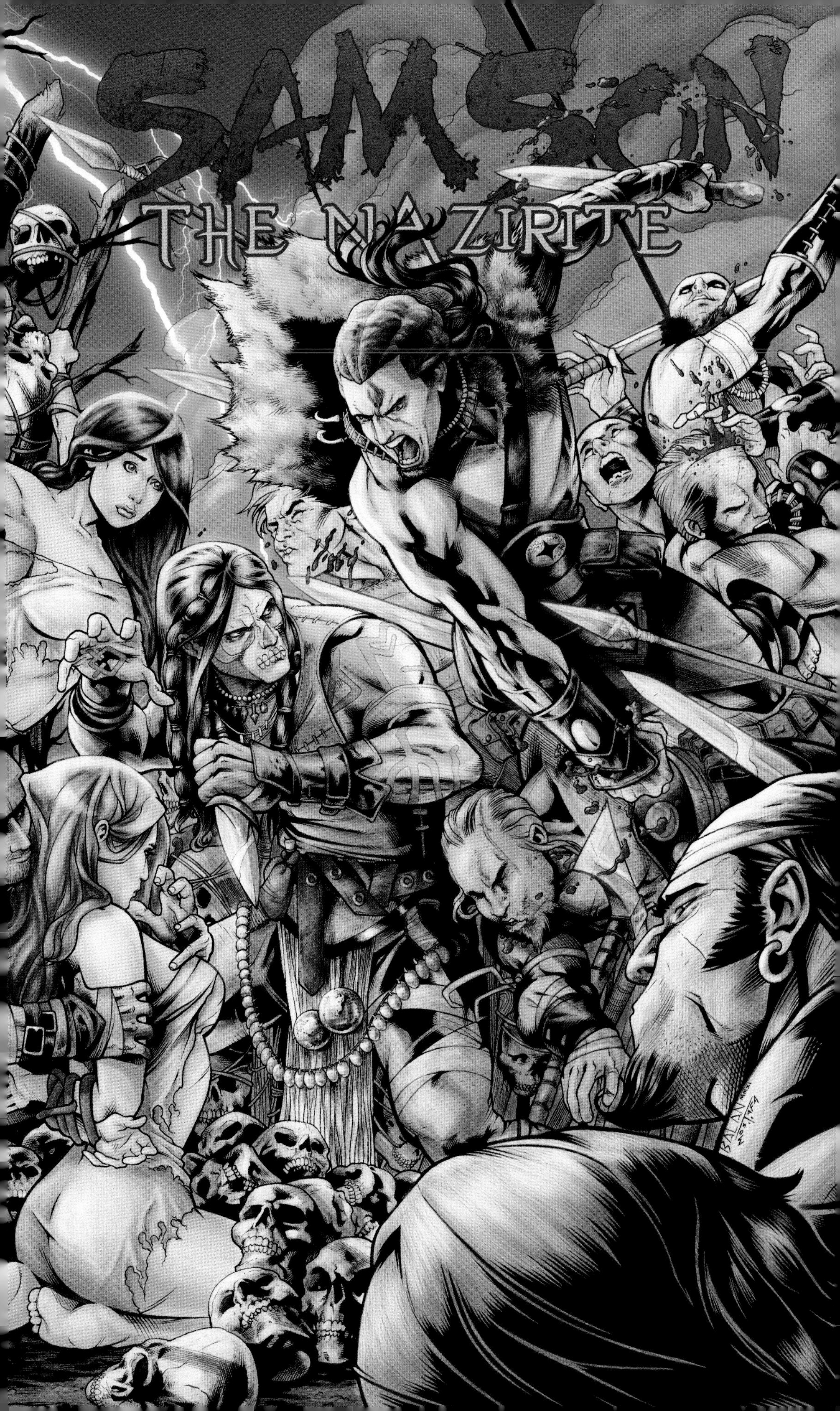
SAMSON
THE NAZIRITE

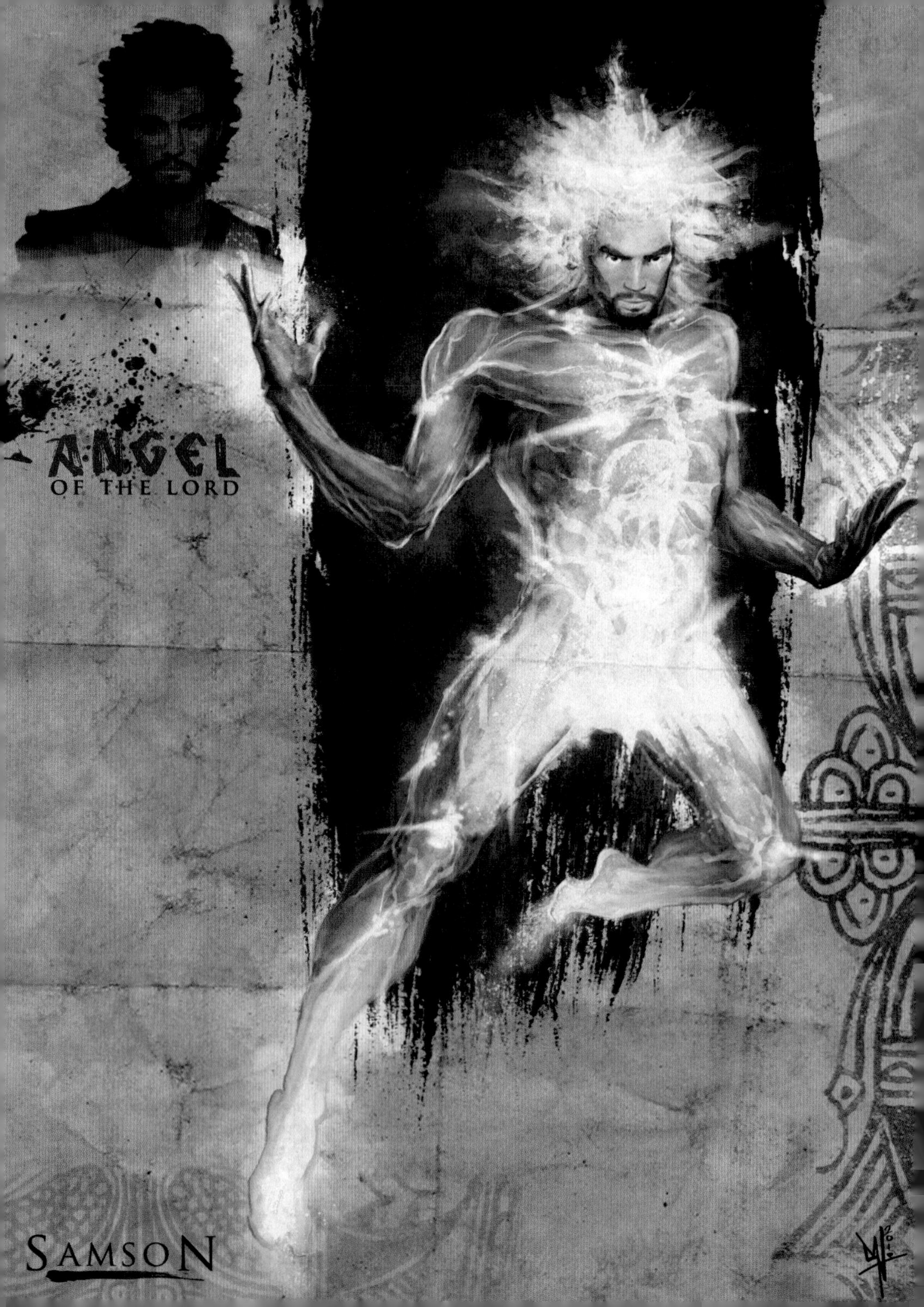
ANGEL
OF THE LORD
SAMSON

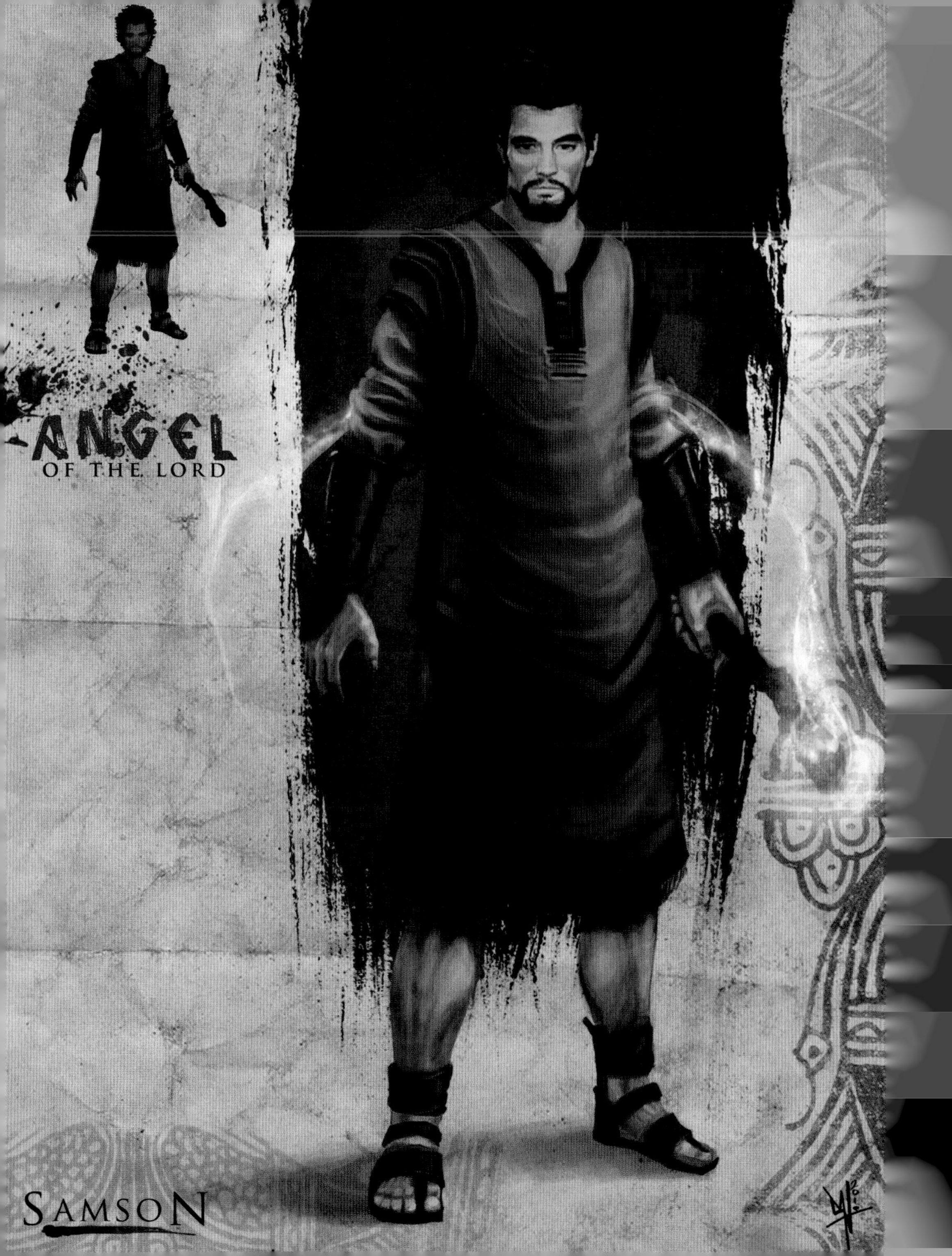
ANGEL
OF THE LORD
SAMSON

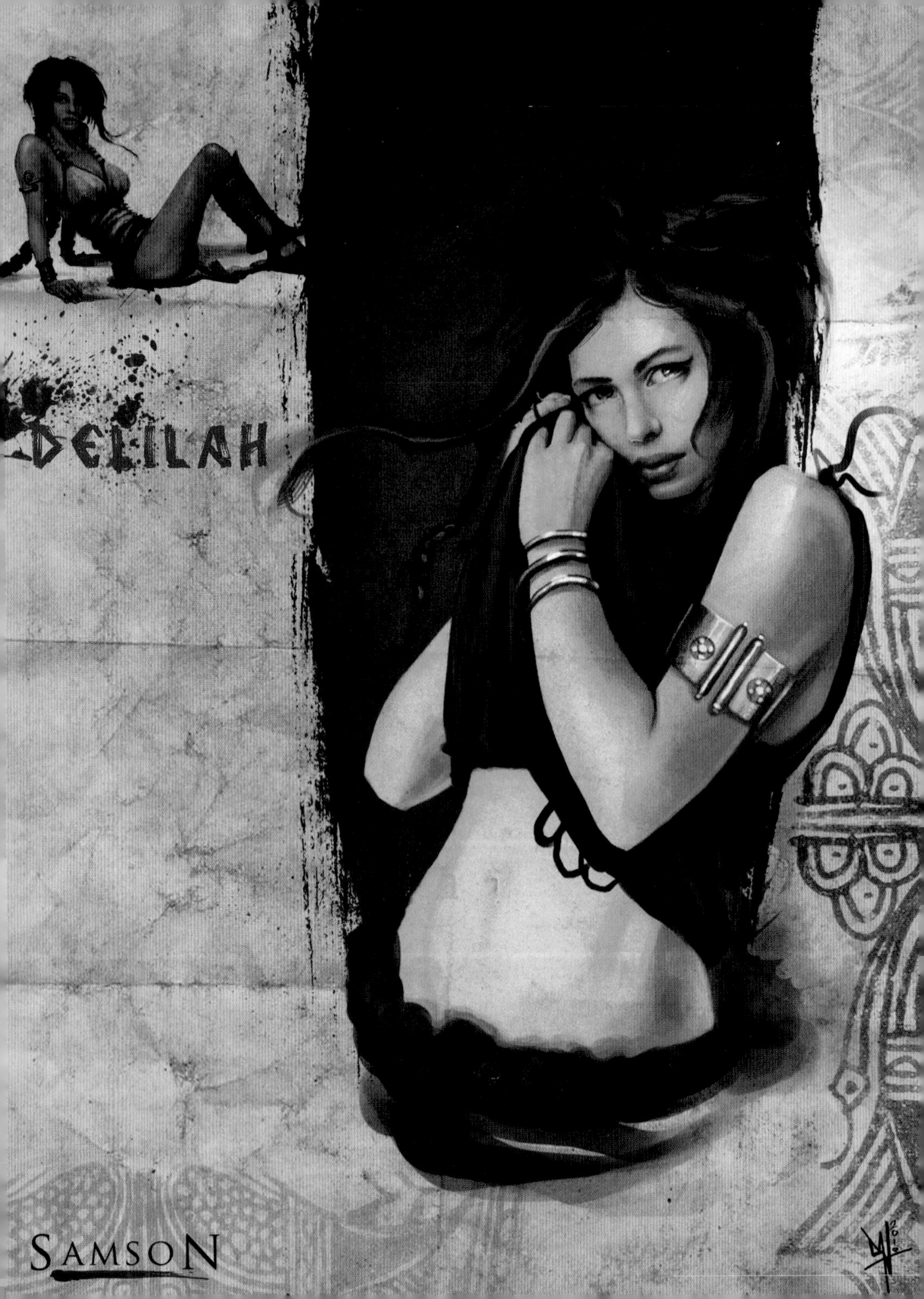
DELILAH
SAMSON